The
WORKMANSHIP
of
LEADERS

Systems, Frameworks, and Information Processing

BOB EMILIANI
Foreword by Steve Tendon

The Workmanship of Leaders: Systems, Frameworks, and Information Processing / Bob Emiliani

Cover design by Bob Emiliani. The human head represents the "knowledge work" of leaders and the overall importance of the head (seeing, hearing, and speaking) in the workmanship of leaders. Back cover photograph by Josh Edenbaum Photography.

ISBN-13: 978-1-7320191-7-1
Library of Congress Control Number: 2023900472

1. Leadership 2. Workmanship 3. Business 4. Sociology
5. Systems 6. Frameworks 7. Information Processing

First Edition: February 2023

Published by Cubic LLC, South Kingstown, Rhode Island, USA.

This publication is believed to provide accurate information with respect to the subject matter covered. It is sold with the understanding that it does not in any way represent legal, financial, business, consulting, or other professional service.

Manufactured using digital print-on-demand technology.

CONTENTS

No AI Generated Text • 100% Human Creativity

Books Series on Leadership

———————————

The Triumph of Classical Management Over Lean Management:
How Tradition Prevails and What to Do About It

Irrational Institutions: Business, Its Leaders,
and The Lean Movement

Management Mysterium: The Quest for Progress

The Aesthetic Compass: Foundation of Leadership
Action and Inaction

A Changed Perspective: An Essential Guide for Emerging Leaders

"One voice is not loud enough to
make institution-level changes."

- Meaghan Roy-O'Reilly

Foreword

Bob Emiliani did it again. He wrote another book! This one you are holding in your hands (or maybe reading off a screen) now. I had just finished reading his book *A Changed Perspective: An Essential Guide for Emerging Leaders*, when I had the pleasure to receive a draft of this one, *The Workmanship of Leaders: Systems, Frameworks, and Information Processing*. This one can be seen as a sequel to the former.

Bob's books are always thought provoking. They will demand your full attention. The signal to noise ratio is incredibly in favor of the signal. Every page has some hidden jewel. Often you will realize the full significance only once you have read along, to discover the full picture, and connect the dots. And then you might want to go back and re-read earlier passages. And what an amazing perspective you will discover then.

So what is it that I find so compelling?

I have been working as a management consultant for over two decades. I've consistently witnessed a pattern in how organizations adopt – only to later abandon – one management approach after another. There is this legend about "management fads." We do not need to name any. I am sure you know more than one. They seem to come and go. None really sticks around.

Why is that? Whether you are a consultant or are in some leadership role in a business, it is a worthwhile question to ponder: Why are such management approaches not persisting?

Political, economic, social, and technological factors keep on changing at an ever-accelerating pace. We all know this. One could believe that this rate of development renders obsolete current management approaches, which are then replaced by newer ones. Generating waves upon waves of such management fads as a way to cope with the ever-changing landscape.

So is that why management approaches need to be replaced, because of obsolescence?

To a certain degree, that must be true. Yet, if we examine, as Bob does in this book, how the structures, policies and decision-making processes employed by leaders shape up, generation after generation, we will discover a common thread. And this common thread is a much more powerful explanation of why management innovations never persist.

Indeed, we can see a common way of dealing with the ever-changing business environment. A way that seems to survive and never really be affected by the latest management fad. It is the power of self-interest that drives managers.

The insight that Bob brings us is, at first, a depressing one. Especially if you work as a management consultant, since you will understand that any effort to change leadership behavior will be in vain! It is also depressing if you are an employee, since you will realize that your conditions will never really become any better. (Yet, bear with me, because there is a light at the end of the tunnel.)

The common factor that spans generations of leaders, going all the way back to prehistoric ages, is a self-serving and self-preserving system of power. A system rooted in traditions and myths. A system made strong with antibodies that resist any deviation or evolution. A system that is stable and long lasting. A system that ultimately leads to what Bob calls the "Institution of Leadership." It is the "System of Profound Privilege."

Bob teaches us that the system is so strongly rooted because it is the path of least resistance for any aspiring leader. Aspiring leaders will acquire it by being exposed to current leaders, via a tacit social learning process, almost through an osmotic process. The system has such a stronghold because it is built on top of preconceptions. They are observed, given, and taught through social conventions.

Preconceptions that do not require any prior experience nor any reasoning! Now, doesn't that sound like an ideal job? You can become a stellar leader without experience and without thinking! In fact many employees endure leadership that seems completely detached from reality and logic.

The disconnect comes about in the clash between preconceptions of leaders and real world facts of employees. They are like cats and dogs, living in parallel realities. When one wags the tail, the other perceives anger. When the other purrs, the first one hears an aggressive growl.

Preconceptions are irreconcilable with real world facts.

Yet the power structure favors the leaders under the spell of their preconceptions. Power structures that give the leaders the upper hand: when things do not turn out as expected, they have a whole company of people to blame for failing.

Since leaders are never truly accountable to the real-world facts, they likewise lose any sense of diligence or conscientiousness – "workmanship," as Bob calls it. The privilege of being right by authority rather than factual elements, dispenses leaders from having to do a good job. There is always some scapegoat to blame, lower down. People are the problem, by design!

Leaders need only care about preserving their rights privileges; with little regard to others, society or the Planet as a whole. At the end, it is all about protecting their own rights and interests; all the while having a sense of spiritual superiority over the pleb of employees. Bob qualifies this generalized abuse as psychological barbarism.

Yes, I said that the findings were depressing.

After reading these thoughts, you will start to despair about ever being able to do anything to counter the Institution of Leadership and the System of Profound Knowledge.

Bob's findings are valuable not only because they provide a way to make sense of what happens with leadership, but also hints at how it can possibly be addressed.

One of the most illuminating passages explains how leaders' preconceptions form beliefs, beliefs drive behaviors, and behaviors produce competencies. The key observation is this: most of contemporary leadership training and development programs aim at changing behaviors. They might have been, at times, an ephemeral success; but their effect is never long lasting. In the long run the overarching strength of the original preconceptions will prevail, the newly acquired behaviors will be dropped, and the old ones will reappear. That is how the system is resistant to change and preserves itself from one generation of leaders to the next.

At the end of his book *A Changed Perspective: An Essential Guide for Emerging Leaders*, Bob exhorted readers to become a new generation of leaders. Leaders oriented toward others, fairness, magnanimity, and sustainability. But there was no real hint of what to do to get there.

In this book, the hint is given. If acting on leaders' behaviors is futile, the implied consequence is that we need to act more at the root: at the level of the beliefs or – even better – the preconceptions that are so dearly held.

We need to favor new preconceptions that will move the focus of leadership attention to considering real facts and logic; that will move the locus of interest from the individual to the system.

Given the state of the world with all the multiple crises hitting us all, I think there is no choice for the leaders of the future, but to embrace this renaissance of illuminated leadership, with leaders that care more about humanity and sustainability.

If they do not, then we will all lose.

I will strive to become such a leader.

Will you too?

Steve Tendon
Managing Director,
TameFlow Consulting Limited
Author of *The Book of TameFlow, Theory of Constraints Applied to Knowledge-Work Management*
February 2023
San Ġiljan, Malta

Preface

Why write a book about the workmanship of leaders? Principally because leader's work is not typically associated with the word "workmanship." So, it seems necessary and worthwhile to explore what leadership would look like if it were thought of as workmanship and if leaders were workmanlike in carrying out their duties. This book explores the meaning of "workmanship" in the context of the work and the function of leadership.

Being a longtime analyst of leaders and leadership – both progressive [1-3] and in the classical tradition [4-8] – my interest is in understanding how leaders think, how they behave, and why they do what they do, given that their work is so consequential to the lives and livelihoods of great numbers of people and to the wellbeing of the planet. The effects that leaders have on followers, both good and bad, are important and far-reaching.

My decades of work experience and research have sought to understand similarities and differences between progressive (new) and classical (old) forms of leadership. In particular, the former, progressive leadership, has more of a sense of workmanship, as the word is commonly understood, compared to classical leadership. Why is that, and what are its ramifications for the evolution of leadership thinking and practice? If progressive leadership is more workmanlike than classical leadership, does that then influence and lead to a more workmanlike practice of classical leadership? Or is workmanship more the exclusive domain of progressive leadership?

Unlike the workers who process material and information by hand, leaders do "knowledge work" and exclusively process information. Leaders use their brain. At any level in an organization, leaders encounter varied forms of information from internal and external sources: employees (subordinates and superiors), texts, emails, internal reports, metrics and KPIs, customers, suppliers, shareholders, consultants, government, media, and so on.

This information, often overwhelming at times, may or may not be checked for accuracy or completeness, or even its meaning. Nevertheless, leaders must process this information to make decisions (or not) and act (or not). What are the frameworks that leaders use to process information? Who is affected by the frameworks, and is it positive or negative?

Additionally, there is the very important matter of leadership development, whether on-the-job, through training and education, or both. What has been the point of focus and has been it been effective? If it is ineffective, why, and what improvements can be made? These are some of the important and interesting questions that this book will engage in search of a much better understanding of leadership. That may, in turn, generate some practical solutions to long-standing problems.

The focus of this book is leaders of for-profit corporations, especially top leaders. However, the subject matter is also applicable to leaders at any level, from supervisor to CEO and board of directors, and for leaders of any type of organization: not-for profit, government, non-governmental organizations, etc. I am certain that leaders in any line of work will find this book to be helpful. At a minimum, it will make you think. My hope is that it will do much more; that it will lead to substantive changes in the understanding and practice of leadership in ways that benefit humanity and our shared habitat, Earth, that gives life to humanity and allows us to survive.

As a prelude to this book, I recommend that you read *A Changed Perspective*" [8], as it will provide needed background information. I hope you enjoy this book and find it interesting and useful.

Bob Emiliani
Wakefield, Rhode Island
February 2023

Trigger Warning: The contents of this book may be upsetting to some people. This book is a technical analysis whose purpose is simply to further understand what is going on [4-8]. It is not an indictment of leaders, leadership, or business. There is no intent to blame or deprecate anyone. Instead, this book simply provides additional insights into and analysis of the Institution of Leadership and the System of Profound Privilege, and thus offers opportunities for improvement. Improvement, however, can look and be different depending on one's social status.

Notes

[1] Emiliani, B. *et al.* (2007), *Better Thinking, Better Results: Case Study and Analysis of an Enterprise-Wide Lean Transformation*, Second Edition, The CLBM LLC, Wethersfield, Connecticut

[2] Emiliani, B. (2009), *Practical Lean Leadership: A Strategic Leadership Guide for Executives*, The CLBM LLC, Wethersfield, Connecticut

[3] Emiliani, M.L. and Emiliani, M. (2013), "Music as a Framework to Better Understand Lean Leadership," *Leadership & Organization Development Journal*, Volume 34, Number 5, pp. 407-426, https://doi.org/10.1108/LODJ-11-0088

[4] Emiliani, B. (2018), *The Triumph of Classical Management Over Lean Management: How Tradition Prevails and What to Do About It*, Cubic LLC, South Kingstown, Rhode Island

[5] Emiliani, B. (2020), *Irrational Institutions: Business, Its Leaders, and The Lean Movement*, Cubic LLC, South Kingstown, Rhode Island

[6] Emiliani, B. (2020), *Management Mysterium: The Quest for Progress*, Cubic LLC, South Kingstown, Rhode Island

[7] Emiliani, B. (2022), *The Aesthetic Compass: Foundation of Leadership Action and Inaction*, Cubic LLC, South Kingstown, Rhode Island

[8] Emiliani, B. (2022), *A Changed Perspective: An Essential Guide for Emerging Leaders*, Cubic LLC, South Kingstown, Rhode Island

Introduction

It is often useful to think of something in a different way to better understand it – to explore its existence, meaning, and boundaries, as well as adjacent and fresh new possibilities. Advancing one's thinking away from the norm, away from the status quo, is more than just a thought experiment. It is an attempt to discover new ground, hopefully coinciding with a time in history where new ground needs to be broken.

We do not normally think of leaders' work in terms of workmanship. But what happens if we do? We might think of leadership differently and develop different expectations of leaders, from supervisor to CEO and the board of directors. We might place different demands on leaders for a different quality and timeliness of their work. Contextualizing the work of leaders as workmanship, rather than as title, role, job, or function can help us better understand what leadership is or what it should be, and how it should evolve over time.

Why is this important? Leadership has been widely studied and written about, resulting in far more useless fluff than useful substance. And there are so many definitions of leadership that it can be almost anything that anyone wants it to be [1]. Most definitions are banalities about having followers and being influential. They are mostly self-regarding (leader focused) rather than other regarding (follower-focused). All of this results in great confusion such that it is far more efficient and remunerative to simply extend, rename, or repackage existing understandings of leadership than it is to break new ground. The effect is to perpetuate traditional conceptualizations of leadership and ignore the need for or creation of new conceptualizations that are a better fit with the times and human needs.

What is workmanship? "Workmanship" is defined as [2]:

- something effected, made, or produced
- the art or skill of a workman
- the quality imparted to a thing in the process of making

There is a clear association with skillfully making something. We normally equate workmanship with hands-on work, especially the type of work that entails craftsmanship – i.e., skillful practice of a trade in the performance of one's job. It might be a toolmaker, artist of some type or another, chef, carpenter, stone mason, knitter, tile setter, potter, etc. Someone whose labor is in the tangible realm of processing materials in a sequence of tasks. We often characterize this as "blue-collar" work, the type of work that suggests a high degree of skill honed through years of on-the-job practice.

To achieve a high degree of skill through daily practice suggests a workmanlike demeanor. What does it mean to be workmanlike? "Workmanlike" is defined as [3]:

- characterized by the skill and efficiency typical of a good workman; workmanlike thoroughness
- competent and skillful but not outstanding or original

"Workmanlike" suggests diligence, attention to details that matter to the overall quality, form, and function of what is being produced. It is the development of progressively greater expertise, skill, and capabilities over time resulting from the daily practice of one's trade.

Both definitions are foreign to the land of leadership. When we think of leaders at any level in an organization – especially top leaders – we typically do not think of their job in terms of workmanship and workmanlike diligence. The work of leaders is "knowledge work" – work that utilizes the mind, not the hands. The work of leaders is information processing – brain work that manifests itself in the form of absorbing information (seeing, hearing, reading), processing information, (thinking, analyzing, drawing conclusions), and producing information (speaking, writing, making decisions), as well as related physical movements (i.e., body language; gestures, facial expressions, eye contact, etc.).

Leaders spend many hours on the job, both at work and at home, and this is generally understood to mean that they work very hard. However, hours worked is not the same thing as workmanship and workmanlike diligence. One can work many hours doing things without workmanship or the workmanlike diligence that is needed to elevate one's skills and capabilities over time. For it is apparent to anyone who has had experience with many leaders that their fundamental ways of thinking and doing things are more similar than different despite their widely varying contexts. If that is workmanship, then it seems to have stalled early in one's leadership training. This further suggests a lack of creativity and an aversion to moving past the status quo.

Additionally, we do not typically think of leadership as a trade or leaders as tradespersons; i.e., people skilled in a craft. Leadership is more commonly understood to be a profession; work that requires specialized knowledge gained through higher education and training. But are leaders professional in the execution of leadership? Leaders, like any human, make lots of small errors and mistakes. But we also know leaders make many significant errors and mistakes that are costly in money and lives, as evident from reading business periodicals such as *The Wall Street Journal* [4] and from compilation and analyses of errors and mistakes [5-7].

Of course, most corporate calamities are never reported in newspapers and are not subject to external study. Therefore, one can correctly conclude that corporate calamities are more common than is generally realized, and that there are significant problems with the workmanship of leaders and associated information processing. Significant errors and mistakes are so prevalent as to be systemic, given that similar types of errors and mistakes are prevalent across companies and industries [6]. The evidence clearly calls for upgrading leadership to higher levels of workmanship [8].

The failure to comprehend leadership as a trade may be partly responsible for the daily run of corporate and organizational calamities. Of course, not all tradespeople perform their work with a high level of professionalism. Yet the consequences of their errors and mistakes are nearly always less costly and far-reaching than the errors and mistakes of senior leaders. How does the firm positioning of leadership as a profession, not as a trade, and leaders as professionals, not as tradespersons, affect their understanding of themselves, their work, and how other see then? It surely sets a low bar with respect to the need to improve one's skills and capabilities, and silences calls from followers for a type of leadership that differs from the norm. Leaders often talk about the importance of quality, pleasing customers, and so on. They also talk of the importance of being attentive to details. As no person can achieve perfection in these matters, it is necessary for them to have a critical eye on the thinking and methods used to produce quality, customer satisfaction, attentiveness to details, etc. Frequently, leaders assume these to be "a given," yet we often find leaders in trouble for poor quality, customer dissatisfaction, and attentiveness to the wrong details. There is a problem with workmanship that lies not just at the level of salaried and hourly laborers, but also at all levels of leadership, from supervisor to the board of directors.

It is generally assumed that the higher one's status, the more skilled and capable a person is. In the trades, a master craftsman has higher status than an apprentice. There is clearly a large gap between the two in terms of experience, skills, and capabilities. In the context of professional leaders, there is likewise a gap between supervisor and CEO. However, the rise to the top of an organization is not necessarily based on experience, skills, and capabilities. In fact, often it is not. Selection committees, even at levels much lower than CEO, place great emphasis on "fit," "chemistry," "gut feel," and numerous assumptions pertaining to technical, business, and social acumen. That this could be a recipe for future disaster is obvious. But more importantly, competition, which normally is expected to result in something better or improved, can have the perverse effect of producing inattentiveness to the workmanship of leaders – by both the individual and the search committee. Attainment of any level of leadership suggests to those chosen that they are good at what they do and that the need to improve must, fundamentally, decrease as their level of status increases. The competitive nature of promotion, especially at senior levels, often means that attaining the position is of much greater importance than developing the workmanship for information processing that avoids corporate calamities.

The fact that humans have survived as a species is remarkable. It is the result of a cumulative development of experience, skills, and capabilities of a quality, efficiency, and effectiveness, necessary for survival. It may even suggest that humans possess an instinct of workmanship that is highly adaptative to changing conditions. Yet top leaders' role requires an understanding of survival that differs from survival of the human species. Generally, the prime directive of top leaders in private enterprise is to create wealth; to make the corporation more valuable and to enrich its owners. Survival of a business is neither preordained nor necessary. A business is a property to be bought or sold when the price is right or shuttered when business conditions turn unfavorable. Corporations are ephemeral, notwithstanding the 5,000 thousand or so (out of several hundred million) that have survived for hundreds of years or more [9]. Under such circumstances, the type and quality of work that leaders do need only be good enough to create wealth for some relatively short period of time. As such, leaders' actual workmanship need only be average, while status conveniently and effortlessly elevates leaders' perceived workmanship to levels of greatness [10]. The long tradition of spiritual adoration of top leaders throws into confusion the reality of their limitations as human beings.

While doing the necessary and good work of satisfying the needs of society, business is a profligate consumer of natural resources and a generator of huge, negative externalities that typically go unaccounted. In normal economic times, there is at least 20 percent more inventory of manufactured, wholesale, and retail goods than sales in the U.S. economy [11], indicating waste and negative externalities accounts for one-fifth of the total good produced and traded [12]. It is likely the same for other economies across the globe. Such waste is not what one would associate with "workmanship" or "workmanlike" diligence. This raises the uncomfortable thought that business, as it has been conducted through the minds of leaders for some time [13], may no longer contribute to human survival in the same way that it once did. Business, along with numerous other related factors, may be detrimental to future human survival, owing to centuries of waste and poor stewardship of the natural resources necessary for life [14] and related path dependencies.

An illustration may help further explain how workmanship is lacking in the work leaders do, particularly in relation to information processing. Figure I-1 shows the range of leaders' response to stimuli in the workplace. The stimuli

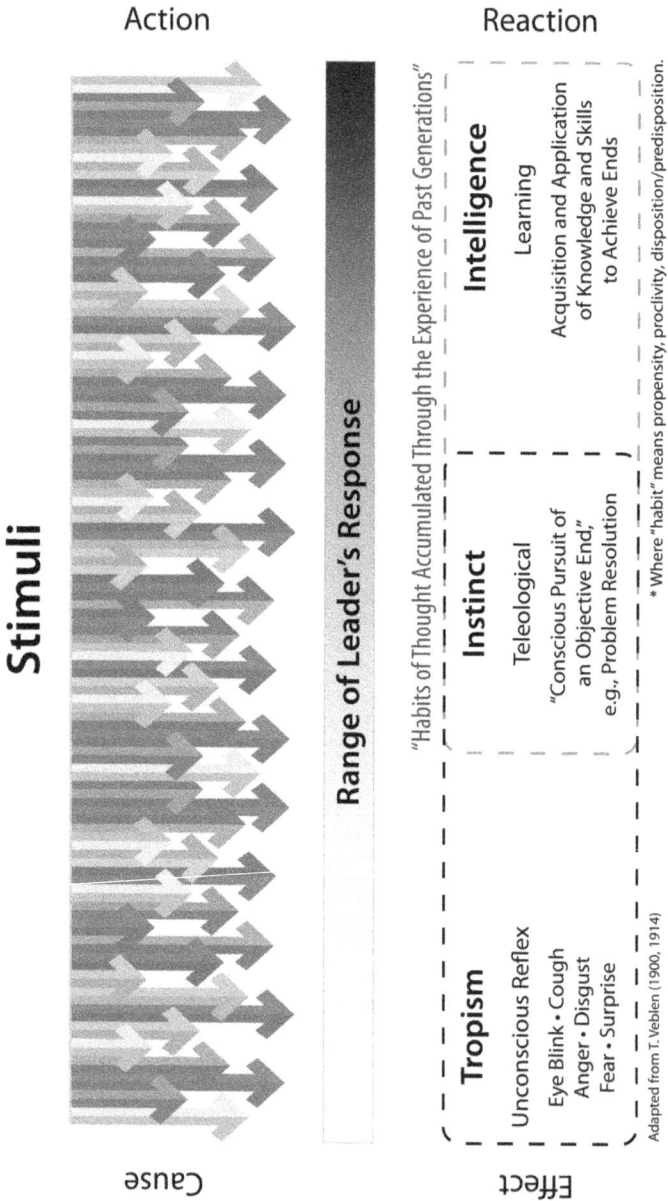

Figure I-1. Range of leader's response to stimuli in the workplace.

would typically be information of one of three varieties: bad news, news, and good news, conveyed orally or in writing. Their response can be tropismatic, instinctive, or intelligent, or some combination of the three. We will take the case of bad news – the emergence of a problem – to illustrate workmanship, for two different top leaders: Leader A and Leader B, both with decades of business experience.

Years of experience have conditioned Leader A to view problems as being intrinsically bad, and bad in relation to the reaction their superior will have if they too become aware of the problem. Upon hearing the bad news, Leader A experiences a millisecond, tropismatic (reflex) response to it; a negative response in terms of facial expression or animated body language and subsequent words spoken. That is immediately followed by an impulse of "How do I fix this problem?" Leader A's tropismatic response is pugnacity; to start yelling or blaming the person who delivered the bad news. There is no workmanship in that. The instinctive reaction to quickly fix the problem is teleological, meaning purposeful effort to make the problem go away. However, fixing the problem and making it go away are two different things. Making a problem go away uses habits of thought and action based upon prior experience by self or others (past generations) – i.e., the use of well-known temporary fixes ("band-aid" solutions; shortcuts) gained through social learning as one ascends the hierarchy. Leader A may do this or specify the corrective action for others to carry out without understanding its actual cause. Either way, there is no workmanship in that. In this case, the use of intelligence is limited to simply making the problem go away quickly. But the problem is never really solved and so it festers until it someday re-emerges, likely in the form of a much bigger problem. These are the costs and consequences of poor or no workmanship.

What does workmanship look like in this example? Upon hearing the bad news, Leader B experiences the same millisecond, tropismatic (reflex) response. But Leader B has learned to suspend judgment and blame, and to avoid animated emotional responses. Leader B stoically deploys their instinct of curiosity to better understand the problem. Leader B asks relevant questions in a non-blaming and non-judgmental way and may even go see the problem for themselves. Next, Leader B applies intelligence in the form of one of the structured problem-solving processes that all leaders have learned some time or another in their careers to identify and correct the root cause(s). Or they may delegate structured problem-solving to other people, coupled with follow-up to positively critique the quality of causal analysis and corrective action. By routinely engaging in structured problem-solving processes, Leader B learns different lessons than Leader A, and in doing so develops greater intelligence and wisdom. This process is illustrative of workmanship and workmanlike diligence towards the end goal of skillfully resolving the problem.

Both types of leaders were faced with the same information processing challenge, yet Leader B exhibited workmanship and workmanlike diligence while Leader A did not. Leader B sets the better example for others in the organization to learn from. Yet most leaders are like Leader A, in part because we demand so little of our leaders – and especially because status magically elevates leaders' perceived workmanship to levels of greatness that do not actually exist. Hence, the ubiquity of corporate calamities that cost people their lives and livelihoods. There are many people like Leader B who fulfill all the other needed qualities and characteristics of being a top leader. Yet most of them are deselected in the promotion processes [15] in favor of Leader A people.

Workmanship and workmanlike diligence can be clearly differentiated between Leader A and Leader B. Both leaders process information and take actions that are designed to fulfill their responsibilities as leaders. Yet Leader As approach has more destructive consequences, especially in terms of the social learning that is being absorbed and put into practice by other leaders lower in the organization. But it is not just information processing that is problematic. It is also the frameworks in which information is processed. That is the subject of Chapter 1, as well as the Leader B deselection phenomenon in promotion processes.

CHAPTER SUMMARY

To engage you, the reader, and improve your learning and
retention, write a short narrative summarizing the
Introduction.

THINK

- What are the one, two, or three things that you do to a high level of skill and expertise at work? Can these things be characterized as great workmanship?

- Do you have great workmanship for things that have little or no meaning or value? How will you correct that?

- What work activities do you engage in with workmanlike diligence?

THINK

- Has your workmanlike diligence been applied to things that matter, or to things that do not really matter? What should you apply workmanlike diligence to?

- How do you typically react to problems? Reflexively negative and in search of quick fixes, or reflexively curious in search of fundamental causes? Whether the former or the latter, who did you learn this from?

Notes

[1] See University of Exeter, Centre for Leadership Studies, (2009), "Leadership Definitions," https://web.archive.org/web/20090310035842/http://www.leadership-studies.com/lsw/definitions.htm, 10 March, accessed 17 January 2023

[2] Definition of "workmanship," https://www.merriam-webster.com/dictionary/workmanship, accessed 17 January 2023

[3] Definition of "workmanlike," https://www.merriam-webster.com/dictionary/workmanlike, accessed 17 January 2023

[4] The errors and mistakes of top leaders are revealed through corporate calamities. Here are a few examples that have occurred in recent years, listed in alphabetical order: Abbott Baby Formula Recalls, Airbus A380 Development, BP Texas Refinery Explosion, P Deepwater Horizon Explosion, Baxter International's Heparin Blood Thinner, Big Pharma's Drug Pipeline Problem in the 2000s, Blue Bell Ice Cream Listeriosis Outbreak, Boeing 787 Development, Bristol-Myers Squibb Accounting Scandal, Champlain Towers Condominium Collapse, Cisco Systems Management Reorganization, Coast Guard's Fast Response Cutter, Compounding Pharmacy Fungal Meningitis, Connecticut Electricity Deregulation, Cost Management in Healthcare, Cost Management in Higher Education, COVID-19 Government Response, Electricity Deregulation, Equifax Data Breach, F-35 Airplane Development, Facebook

Election Disinformation Crisis, Fall of Lehman Brothers, Merrill Lynch, etc., Fisker Automotive Bankruptcy, Fisher-Price Baby Sleeper, Flint Lead Water Contamination, General Motors Bankruptcy, General Motors Ignition Switch, Greensill Capital Failure, Grenfell Tower Fire, HMRC Lean Transformation Failure, JC Penney Financial Distress, Johnson & Johnson Talc Baby Powder, Johnson & Johnson OTC Drug Recalls, Koninklijke Ahold N.V. Financial Scandal, KraftHeinz Private Equity Mismanagement, Microsoft OS Product Failures, Minerals Management Service Failed Oversight, Morandi Bridge Collapse, Morcellator Medical Device Failure, Mylan EpiPen Price Scandal, Nestle Noodles India Contamination, Opioid Epidemic, Pacific Gas & Electric Fires, Peanut Corporation of America Salmonella Recall, Peloton Treadmill Recall, Pratt & Whitney PW 6000 Engine, Privatization of Public Assets, Rare Earths Price Bubble, Rite Aid Bankruptcy, Simmons Bedding Company, Southwest Airlines December 2022 Meltdown, Sunbeam Bankruptcy, Synthes Bone Cement, Takata Airbags, Tax Breaks for Tech Companies, Texas Winter Power Outage, Timken Company Spinoff, Toyota Early 2000s Quality Problems, U.S. Government Future Imagery Spy Satellite, Vale Mining Disaster, Valeant Pharmaceutical Drug Pricing, Warnaco Bankruptcy, Wells Fargo Fraud, Xerox Y2K Near-Bankruptcy. If you do not know of these corporate calamities, Google them. Of course, most corporate calamities are never reported in the newspaper. Therefore, one can correctly conclude that there are significant problems with the workmanship of leaders and associated information processing. See Notes 5, 6, and 7.

[5] Emiliani, B. (2015), *Speed Leadership: A New Way to Lead for Rapidly Changing Times*, The CLBM LLC, Wethersfield, Connecticut

[6] Emiliani, B. and Torinesi, M. (2021), *Wheel of Fortune: Getting to the Heart of Business Strategy*, Cubic LLC, South Kingstown, Rhode Island

[7] Emiliani, B. (2023), *A Changed Perspective: An Essential Guide for Emerging Leaders*, Cubic LLC, South Kingstown, Rhode Island

[8] That is the purpose of this book, as well as the books cited in Notes 5, 6, and 7, is to upgrade the workmanship of leaders.

[9] For a list of the world's oldest businesses, see https://en.wikipedia.org/wiki/List_of_oldest_companies. "Of the companies with more than 100 years of history, most of them (89%) employ fewer than 300 people."

[10] Gelles, D. (2022), *The Man Who Broke Capitalism: How Jack Welch Gutted the Heartland and Crushed the Soul of Corporate America – And How to Undo His Legacy*, Simon & Schuster, New York, New York

[11] United States Census Bureau, "Manufacturing and Trade Inventories and Sales: Inventories to Sales Ratio" https://www.census.gov/econ/currentdata/dbsearch?progr amCode=MTIS&startYear=1992&endYear=2019&categori es[]=TOTBUS&dataType=SM&geoLevel=US&adjusted=1

&notAdjusted=1&errorData=0, accessed 19 January 2023

[12] "World Data: The World's Largest Economies," https://www.worlddata.info/largest-economies.php, accessed 18 January 2023

[13] A date marking this inflection point might be the early 19th century, the early 20th century, or the early 21st century, depending upon one's viewpoint or the facts.

[14] Penuelas, J. *et al.* (2022), "Increasing Divergence Between Human and Biological Elementomes," *Trends in Ecology & Evolution*, Volume 37, Number 11, pp. 935-938, DOI: 10.1016/j.tree.2022.08.007eye.html, accessed 18 January 2023

[15] A notable exception is H. Lawrence Culp Jr., Chairman and Chief Executive Officer of GE and Chief Executive Officer of GE Aerospace, https://www.ge.com/about-us/leadership/profiles/lawrence-culp, accessed 18 January 2023

1

Systems and Frameworks

To understand how top leaders process information, we must first examine the systems under which they exist. To do that, we must understand how preconceptions inform leaders' thinking and decisions. We will define "preconception" as a preconceived opinion or idea *formed prior to experience*; a prejudice or bias; the *absence of reasoning* [1]. Figure 1-1 shows that at any point in time, say from the Bronze Age forward, there exists a Human Supersystem of Preconceptions (HSP) in various stages of advancement or regression. These inform the Organizational Macrosystem of Preconceptions (OMP) that people are part of. This, in turn informs the Individual Microsystem of Preconceptions (IMP) [2] that guides people's day-to-day thinking and actions.

Preconceptions are a type of intelligence, P-intelligence, that interacts with fact-based intelligence, F-intelligence. P-intelligence can dominate F-intelligence because it is easily passed from one generation to the next through family, school, work, church, etc., and thus is long-lived. Furthermore, it is very difficult to refute traditions swiftly and cleanly, and there is inherent difficulty in challenging the "ruling class of elders." Inferiors arguing with superiors is characteristically preordained to be a losing cause. F-Intelligence can, over time, replace various elements of P-intelligence, but F-intelligence can never completely replace P-intelligence. A significant amount of P-intelligence exists whether one likes it or not. They dynamic interplay between these two types of intelligence constitute one's overall intelligence at any point in time.

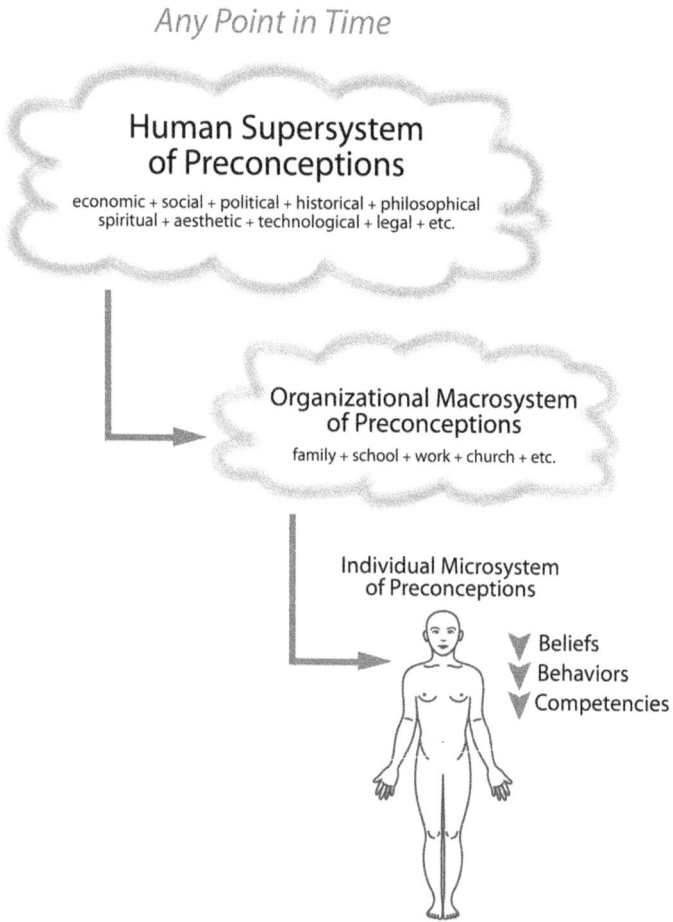

Figure 1-1. Cascading systems of preconceptions – HSP, OMP, and IMP systems. The supersystem (HSP) contains at least nine categories of preconceptions, with each category containing ten or more preconceptions that guide information processing [3].

In the case of top leaders, they are members of what I have

previously described as the Institution of Leadership (leaders' social habits of thought and action) and the System of Profound Privilege (the vested rights and interests that leaders protect and preserve) [4]. These are constituted with numerous and varied traditions that have been passed down for thousands of years. These traditions are typically more P-intelligence – *formed prior to experience* and in the *absence of reasoning* – than F-intelligence, which is based on experience and reasoning. The basis for information processing thus differs in relation to one's P-intelligence and F-intelligence and leads to great variation in how people understand problems and how they think problems should be solved.

The cascading progression of preconceptions shown for IMP in Figure 1-1 can be expressed as:

Preconceptions → Beliefs → Behaviors → Competencies

Thus, preconceptions inform leaders beliefs which informs their behaviors which informs their competencies. This process can produce undesirable behaviors and undesirable competencies (workmanship) as was the case for Leader A (Introduction, pp. 9-11). Most, if not nearly all leadership training and development is directed towards behaviors. This is the primary point of intervention. But as is apparent from Figure 1-1, there is much that precedes behaviors that goes unaddressed when the focus of improvement is leadership behaviors.

When the focus of leadership training and development is behaviors, it unavoidably isolates people from the larger systems that they exist in. It isolates individuals as if they are homogeneous globules and blames them for their failings (Figure 1-2). And so, the only one who can fix it is you. Training to improve leadership behaviors does not address the Individual Microsystem of Preconceptions (IMP), let alone the Organizational Macrosystem of Preconceptions (OMP) or the Human Supersystem of Preconceptions (HSP). They remain unchanged. And that explains why training to improve leadership behaviors, despite its multi-decade commercial success and the fact that participants find it interesting if not entertaining, fails to produce meaningful changes in leadership behaviors. The Institution of Leadership and the System of Profound Privilege, rooted in HSP, continue to prevail.

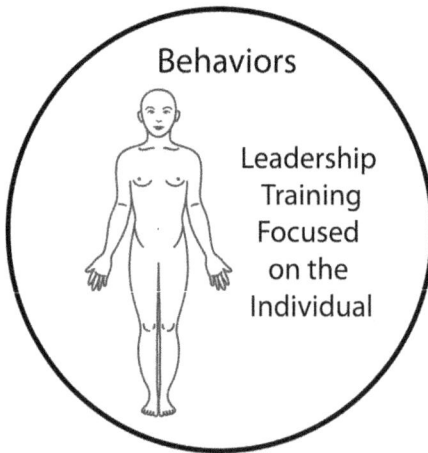

Figure 1-2. Training focused on individuals as isolated homogeneous globules in need of improvement.

Leaders lead more or less in the ways they always have, with physical barbarism being mostly replaced by psychological barbarism [5]. Common examples of psychological barbarism include blaming people for problems, fear of job (and income) loss, gaslighting, microaggressions, unknown expectations, bias, stereotypes, inconsistency, misleading, micromanaging, bullying, public humiliation, dishonesty, disrespect, closed-mindedness, condescension, intimidation, retaliation, hypocrisy, chronic stress, bad metrics and KPIs, bureaucracy, turf wars, backstabbing, budget games, hoarding information, and so on. These behaviors disrupt or cut off the flow of information to leaders which in turn intensifies these negative behaviors and eventually results in corporate calamity. Psychological barbarism is connected to physical barbarism in that over the long-term it will produce various types of health problems for workers (and likely family problems as well). To be clear, not all leaders do these things – perhaps it is better to say they do not think they do these things. Some leaders are overt in these behaviors, while others are more covert. Regardless, these are long-time features of the Institution of Leadership and the System of Profound Privilege. They are tradition, designed to compel people to do what leaders want them to do.

In the case of both training to improve leadership behaviors and how leaders treat people, the individual frame, or I-frame is used to solve the problem [6, 7]. In fact, the I-frame, individual-level solutions, are used to solve most system-level, S-Frame, problems. But obviously, solving the problem at the individual level does not solve problems that exist at the system level – HSP, especially, and OMP. Solving the problem at the system level means changes in preconceptions. The Institution of Leadership and the

System of Profound Privilege have proven themselves adept over vast stretches of time at resisting such change, and followers, demanding little of leaders, largely accept the status quo. Those with vested interests, such as top leaders who enjoy numerous rights and privileges, are keen to preserve the status quo. This can be done most effectively by proffering I-frame solutions to S-frame problems, e.g., worker training. Most leaders will participate in I-frame solutions to improve leadership behaviors, knowing explicitly or implicitly that IMP, OMP, and S-frame (HSP) will not be changed.

They will learn a few useful things from behaviors-based training, and some skills-based training as well as they ascend the hierarchy, but their vested interests and their rights and privileges will be unaffected (HSP). The most important learning is social learning – what they learn from their leaders in person or by reputation – not classroom or experiential training sessions. Importantly, top leaders, learn that they are inheritors of ancient honorable traditions that they, knowingly or not, are obligated to pass on to others, and will work to fulfill their obligations and thus strengthen the S-frame. These efforts may not be fully intentional, but they nevertheless do reflect a collective high level of workmanship and workmanlike diligence that they see as worth preserving [8]. Thus, leaders' workmanship and workmanlike diligence are applied to an end that differs from the common understanding of leadership which is to guide or direct organizations.

Individual-level failings are comprehensively rejected by those highest in the Natural Social Order [9], while the fallibility of those lower in the Natural Social Order are readily accepted, from the level of society on down to the infirm (Table 1-1). This occurs by a process wherein people high in status consistently send the message of individual failings which, over time, becomes incorporated into the common sense of the community. The Natural Social Order conveniently aligns with the Natural Rights and the free market to consistently produce the economic, social, and political outcomes favorable to the interests of those highest in status. That should be no surprise, though the level of economic, social, and political disparity (e.g., income distribution, wealth concentration) oscillates over time.

Table 1-1 The Natural Social Order

Monarchs
Business Leaders
Politicians
Society
Groups
Individuals
Customers
Suppliers
Labor Unions
Salaried Labor
Hourly Labor
Poor
Indolent
Infirm

Presently, the level of economic disparity in America rivals the Gilded Age (circa 1877 to 1900). However, it is not all gloom and doom. Sound arguments can be made regarding humanity's material progress since the Bronze Age, though with the greatest benefits flowing consistently to those highest in the Natural Social Order throughout that expanse of time, current day included. It is true that even incompetent or ruthless leaders (some, anyway) find the wherewithal to do some overall good [10]. Reality is not designed to please everyone regardless of their position in the Natural Social Order.

But there is always room for improvement, and therein lies the perpetual tension between high and low status groups. Top leaders rarely, if ever, speak of the "nobility of labor" or the "dignity of work," to elevate work, celebrate it, and respect it. That is because historically, nobility is based on moral and spiritual superiority and the exploitation and denigration of productive (i.e., slave, serf, and wage) labor. Work is seen by those at the top of the Natural Social Order as drudgery, vulgar and ignoble; as having no prestige, honor, or dignity. There is, however, honor in leading conflict, conspicuous consumption, and dominating other people. Clearly, labor has a huge historical disadvantage and the I-frame approach to correct human failings (e.g., training courses, nudges, incentives) is instrumental in perpetuating the status quo – to negate S-frame change that the mass of workers churn for since at least the Bronze Age (5000-plus years ago).

Those high in the Natural Social Order exhibit workmanship and workmanlike discipline in their efforts to reframe S-frame problems to I-frame problems. People lower in the Natural Social Order who accept I-frame interventions – which is most people – inadvertently relieve pressure on those high in the Natural Social Order for systemic changes. This effectively deletes S-frame solutions to economic, social, and political problems – HSP-based problems – that are well understood and could be easily corrected. This creates formidable obstacles to needed progress.

The idea that individual responsibility can best solve S-frame problems such as global warming, as opposed to systemic reform, require the combined efforts of billions of people, individual efforts that are similar in scope, magnitude, consistency, and duration. Such an occurrence is unlikely [11]. Efforts to individualize, to I-frame most things, seems to benefit individuals, but the actual beneficiary accrues to those at the top of the Natural Social Order. Atomizing society greatly weakens challenges to authority. It increases self-regarding proclivities among the population which substantially reduces other-regarding proclivities (e.g., sharing, teamwork, and sacrifice).

On a smaller scale, company-sponsored training seems to be a good thing; a vote of confidence in the person and a pathway for advancement. Sending a vice president to a training session designed to improve leadership behaviors, whether independently or together with their peer group, is highly unlikely to produce systemic change within the organization, let alone the ancient Institution of Leadership and the System of Profound Privilege. Such training is well known to have little or no lasting effect. We just do not like to admit it or say it out loud. And we are starved for better solutions to this problem, which seems intractable based on the current common understanding of leadership and human resource development. Relatedly, organizational design, as expressed by the typical hierarchical organization chart, plays an important role in making sure that people are the problem; that weakness, fallibility, and failure are the sole responsibility of the individual who does not measure up.

By maintaining a focus on leadership behaviors, and individual weakness (blaming yourself), it precludes paying attention to the major causal factors that contribute to the problem. Framing solutions in terms of individual (personal) responsibility and individual action leave open the likelihood of individual irresponsibility and individual inaction. Hoping for a better world through personal responsibility and individual efforts diverts attention from needed S-frame reforms. Such interventions move away from the I-frame realm of psychology and economics (both classical and behavioral) to the socio-political realm where it belongs. There is, however, much that those high in the Natural Social Order are loathe to lose by doing that. What might be gained is not evident based on the current formulation of HSP (P-intelligence).

It is ironic that people can be so easily manipulated in such ways to reinforce the status quo, severely limit one's agency, and put the core human interests of individuals and society so far out of reach [12]. We are told that struggling alone builds character. That is nice. But what else of consequence does it build? Overall, the workmanship of leaders and associated information processing is directed more towards preserving the status quo – the Institution of Leadership and the System of Profound Privilege – than it is towards improving the work and function of leadership in relation to the wants and needs of followers or of society. To the extent that leaders exhibit workmanship in this lesser realm, it is likely to be perfunctory, only on an as-needed basis, and strictly limited to what the top leader is willing to give [13].

This chapter has sought to prove the folly of training whose focus is to improve leadership behaviors. It is folly because the underlying preconceptions – HSP, OMP, and IMP (the P-intelligence) – go unchanged. The behavior training is F-intelligence based, and therefore often has little practical meaning or use in organizations whose common sense is defined mostly by the P-intelligence coming from top leaders. I-frame solutions do little or nothing to change or improve systemic problems. Yet because of widespread endorsement of the I-frame by leaders, trainers, consultants, teachers, and others have unwittingly bought into the I-frame as a solution to problems that properly belong in the S-frame and which require S-frame interventions. This leaves us in a bit of a conundrum. We will explore how deep a conundrum in the next chapter.

Finally, the Introduction spoke briefly about the promotion process and who gets selected (Leader A) and who gets deselected (Leader B). Consideration of candidates for promotion to jobs such as supervisor or mid-level manager are based primarily on technical skills, with social skills increasing in importance post-promotion to supervisor. After that, promotion to lower and higher executive levels begin to take into consideration intangible factors that weigh more heavily in top leaders' decisions to promote someone. These are the traditional metaphysical "fit," "chemistry," and "gut feel" criteria, as well as numerous assumptions pertaining to technical, business, and social acumen (i.e., competence in money-making, getting things done, defending the organization, or eagerness to please, whichever are needed most). Part of this judgment centers on who will best support the Institution of Leadership and the System of Profound Privilege. Who can be expected to best fulfill their sacred obligations to current and future leaders: the traditionalist (the institutionalist), or the free thinker? The answer is, of course, obvious [14].

CHAPTER SUMMARY

To engage you, the reader, and improve your learning and retention, write a short narrative summarizing Chapter 1.

THINK

- Draw a sketch showing the relationship between P-Intelligence and F-Intelligence as a function of one's status in an organization (low to high status).

- How has your mind and body reacted as a recipient of "psychological barbarism?"

THINK

- In the context of your company or department, identify S-frame problems that were transformed into I-frame problems.

- Regarding social learning, identify some important lessons that you learned from your boss about leadership soon after you were hired into your first job.

THINK

- Assuming the Natural Social Order is fixed for the calculable future, what could be done to return I-frame problems to their appropriate S-frame?

Notes

[1] Preconceptions can be thought of as a type of human "source code" that guides how people think and work. Or, perhaps as the "hardware" architecture on which the operating system (beliefs) run to execute the software program (behaviors) that generate the outputs (competencies).

[2] Funnily enough, "IMP" can be a homonym for the word "imp," a small mischievous devil. People can, at times, be just that, or more. https://en.wikipedia.org/wiki/Imp, accessed 19 January 2023

[3] For a comprehensive exposition on preconceptions, see Emiliani, B. (2023), *A Changed Perspective: An Essential Guide for Emerging Leaders*, Cubic LLC, South Kingstown, Rhode Island

[4] See the three-volume series: Emiliani, B. (2018), *The Triumph of Classical Management Over Lean Management: How Tradition Prevails and What to Do About It*, Cubic LLC, South Kingstown, Rhode Island; Emiliani, B. (2020), *Irrational Institutions: Business, Its Leaders, and The Lean Movement*, Cubic LLC, South Kingstown, Rhode Island; and Emiliani, B. (2020), *Management Mysterium: The Quest for Progress*, Cubic LLC, South Kingstown, Rhode Island

[5] McCleary, R. (2023), "The Man Who Tried to Stop the Space Shuttle Challenger's Launch," *The Wall Street Journal*, 27 January, https://www.wsj.com/articles/the-man-who-tried-

to-stop-the-challenger-launch-space-shuttle-exploration-rob
ert-boisjoly-moral-injury-11674857494, accessed 27 January
2023

[6] Chater, N. & Loewenstein, G. (2022). "The i-frame and
the s-frame: How focusing on individual-level solutions has
led behavioral public policy astray." *Behavioral and Brain
Sciences*, https://doi.org/10.1017/S0140525X22 002023.

[7] One can also think of the I-frame as representing a thing
or object, while the S-frame represents process. See Koskela,
L.J. and Kagioglou, M. (2005), "On the Metaphysics of
Production," *13th International Group for Lean Construction
Conference*, 19-21 July 2005, Sydney, Australia. https://usir.
salford.ac.uk/id/eprint/9378/. Business leaders who focus
on thing prevent process problems (system problems) from
getting solved.

[8] Examples of this form of workmanship and workmanlike
diligence are far too numerous to list, but here are two such
examples: Fahrenthold, D., and Smith, T. (2023) "How
Restaurant Workers Help Pay for Lobbying to Keep Their
Wages Low," *The New York Times*, 17 January,
https://www.nytimes.com/2023/01/17/us/politics/restaur
ant-workers-wages-lobbying.html, accessed 19 January 2023,
and Weber, L. (2023), "FTC Plan to Ban Noncompete
Clauses Shifts Companies' Focus," *The Wall Street Journal*,
https://www.wsj.com/articles/ftc-plan-to-ban-noncompete
-clauses-shifts-focus-to-deferred-pay-nondisclosure-agreeme
nts-11673904728

[9] The unusual term "Natural Social Order" is used because it is both more specific and pertinent to the arguments put forth in this volume. There is nothing in Nature that requires this to be the human social order. Thus, it is "natural" only in the sense of custom or tradition. As time passes, this social order has become more of a choice than a requirement.

[10] Frazer, J.G. (1905), *Lectures on the Early History of the Kingship*, Macmillan and Co., Limited, London, United Kingdom

[11] Which is not to say the I-frame should never be put to use. Solutions to big problems require combinations of S-frame and I-frame solutions, with most solutions weighted towards the S-frame.

[12] As a reminder, most people possess a systematic bias to place their faith in business leaders (more so than political leaders). They give business leaders (and other authority figures) the benefit of the doubt in matters that affect them or others. In doing so, we underappreciate or neglect the pervasiveness of manipulation. Systematic bias can be reduced by increasing one's awareness of it – by looking for it.

[13] You would likely do the same thing if you were in their shoes.

[14] Social learning whose aim is conformist forces a reduction in cultural variation. Status, language, job function, and other factors signal membership in the group (the

Institution of Leadership). Concurrently, this intensifies the differences that exist between institutionalist and free-thinking groups. These differences result in intergroup conflict, either overly or through passive-aggressive behaviors. Demands for obedience to authority further intensifies differences which lead to reduced cooperation and productivity.

2

Negentropic Systems

You have probably heard of the word "entropy." It originated in the scientific study of losses that occur in motive power (e.g., machines) and became integral to the second law of thermodynamics. "Entropy" is derived from Greek to mean "transformation" and represents a state of disorder or randomness [1]. Qualitatively, entropy means the tendency of systems to become disordered, random, or chaotic (loss of energy). For example, the entropy of the universe tends to a maximum, and the increase of disorder is what distinguishes past from present and present from future. In this way, entropy gives us the direction of time; the one-way arrow of time leading to disorder.

A much less familiar term is "negentropy," a *portmanteau* of the words "negative" and "entropy" [2]. Negentropy is the reverse of entropy, and a thing becomes more ordered rather than less ordered. It becomes more organized and takes on shape and structure. This enables the establishment of a function of whatever the thing happens to be. Life is negentropic because it involves an increase in order; the ordering of molecules into cells and cells into a human body, or the conversion of food into nutrients that provide energy to our bodies to avoid decay. Negentropy does not last forever. It is temporary. Eventually, living things die whether on a cellular level or as a human being or other animal.

Social systems are also negentropic because they convert

disorder to order and result in functions that are useful. Government (believe it or not) is a negentropic social system, a conglomeration of social functions whose work is to serve the interests and needs of a society. Business, categorized as a social science by academics, is a social system, also negentropic. Companies take varied types and forms of disorder and through specialized functions transform material and information to produce products and services that people need or desire. Companies are temporary, as are all social systems, but they can be long-lived.

Leadership and followers constitute a negentropic social system. Leaders change periodically, resulting in changes to the social system, sometimes for better and sometimes for worse. While leaders and followers eventually die, they are swiftly replaced so that the social system continues to live on. Civilizations survive because of negentropy [3]. In some cases, the prior civilization and social system is no longer recognizable and replaced with something entirely different. The ancient Egyptian empire lasted for 30 centuries until its conquest by Alexander the Great, and the transformed social systems that survive are present-day Egypt, Sudan, Cyprus, Lebanon, Syria, Israel and Palestine (the latter being former conquered territories).

This brings us to the special case of the Institution of Leadership and the System of Profound Privilege. It is a negentropic social system; a living system of top leaders who come and go over time, closely aligned in their social habits of thought and action and interest in protecting and preserving their vested rights and interests. If you were elevated to the position of CEO and became part of that social system, it is near-certain that you would rapidly absorb its teachings and points of view (P-intelligence) through social learning processes, and you would perpetuate it as others before you have. When you retired or got fired, your replacement would do the same. And on it goes. New leaders feed off (i.e., "metabolize") the preconceptions of prior generations of leaders. This process begins long before becoming CEO, at the start of one's first job through the social learning process with their boss and subsequent bosses.

Negentropy explains why the Institution of Leadership and the System of Profound Privilege is so long-lived and why it continues to thrive. Leaders of different organizations, caliber, and duration in office are the life that has kept it going since ancient times, and perhaps even since the late period of prehistory. Leaders keep it alive by brute force, shows of strength and fortitude, and by gentle guiding hands to assure it remains functional to deliver the required authority, freedom, entitlements, advantages, opportunities, rights, and benefits, and to limit unwanted disruptions to the status quo. These requirements are embedded in the Human Supersystem of Preconceptions (HSP) and flow through the Organizational Macrosystem of Preconceptions (OMP) and finally into the Individual Microsystem of Preconceptions (IMP) of leaders.

In this respect, leaders' self-regarding workmanship in the creation, maintenance, and improvement of the Institution of Leadership and the System of Profound Privilege is that of a master craftsman, remarkable in its longevity and durability.

Conversely, leaders' other-regarding workmanship is poor, principally because those lower in the Natural Social Order are seen as being morally and spiritually inferior and thus not deserving of anything more or better than what they already get. Leaders' workmanship and workmanlike diligence is directed more towards the preserving the Institution of Leadership and the System of Profound Privilege (S-frame) than individual survival (I-frame). Other-regarding workmanship, generally being poor due to the S-frame focus, limits leaders' term in office, which, in addition to being acceptable to most leaders [4] is also inevitable.

The consequences of this are profound for the leadership development services provided by trainers, internal and external consultants, coaches, and educators – particularly the ever-popular behavior, ethics, and similar "soft skills" training programs; e.g. Myers-Briggs, emotional intelligence, authenticity, coaching, and numerous other programs. It suggests that most such training is useless or nearly so. And that may extend to adjacent training programs for diversity, equity, and inclusion (DEI); environmental, social, and governance (ESG); and effective altruism. The social system and social learning process of top leaders result in a common viewpoint that disfavors such training, though they endure it for the purpose of good appearances and a show of compliance.

You may say, "Don't we already know that most of that training is useless? Yes, we do. Legendary are the anecdotes of leaders going away for training and then returning to work with new behaviors and skills to put into practice. The training initially looks to have done some good, but after a few weeks the leaders returns to their previous ways of thinking, behaving, and doing things. The difference is that we now know why.

The Institution of Leadership and the System of Profound Privilege evades decay, significant decay at least, because it is an open system, one that can exchange energy and matter with its surroundings. Closed systems (e.g., a light bulb) cannot do that and so entropy increases. The "order-from-disorder" phenomenon can only occur in open systems. The Institution of Leadership and the System of Profound Privilege is an ordered system, and it is simple [5], not complex and unordered, because it is directed towards achieving the basic function of perpetuating leaders' social habits of thought and action and protecting and preserving their vested rights and interests. There are clear cause-and-effect relationships. It is survival in its most elemental form. Its openness, order, and simplicity are what give the Institution of Leadership and the System of Profound Privilege its enduring strength and durability. Training to improve leadership behaviors cannot upset that.

Figure 2-1 depicts the simple and ordered negentropic system of a leader (left) and a training course to improve leadership behaviors (right). From the perspective of the trainer, training to improve leadership behaviors is seen as bringing order to disorder – i.e., the haphazard way in which leaders typically behave. From the perspective of the leader (i.e., the negentropic system), the leadership behaviors training is a dose of entropy that has the potential to introduce disorder that might interfere with the basic function of perpetuating leaders' social habits of thought and action and protecting and preserving their vested rights and interests. The ordered system either rejects the training outright or it absorbs and negates it either wholly or in part. A few remnants perceived

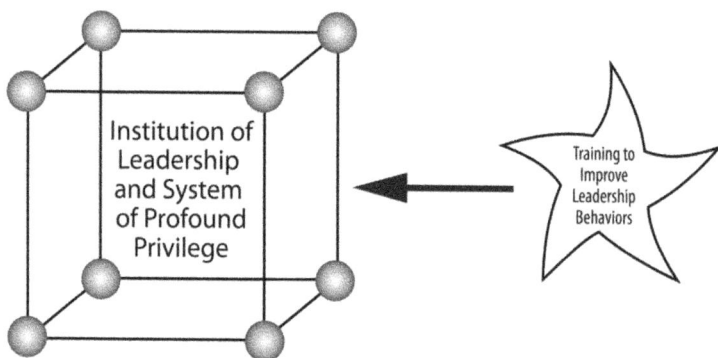

Figure 2-1. Disordered entropic leadership training seeking to penetrate an ordered negentropic system. It will be absorbed into the ordered system and negated in whole or part.

by leaders as useful to the basic function of the Institution of Leadership and the System of Profound Privilege may survive. It is leaders' prerogative to accept or reject any or all parts of any training, coaching, or educational experience.

Behavior and other soft skills leadership training is entropic because it definitionally disorganized – i.e., there are scores of ways to define good leadership [6]. These same definitions can be used to describe bad leadership. This is ideal for the business of leadership training and development because there is no right answer and thus no specific end or goal. From the perspective of trainers, consultants, and educators, leadership is seen as a complex, if not chaotic activity that needs to be tamed through various training and development interventions. However, the Institution of Leadership and the System of Profound Privilege are the strong force, while training to improve leadership behaviors is the weak force – a very weak force. Consequently, forms of leadership desired by followers, such as servant leadership, go largely unheeded.

What else goes unheeded? The various efforts to improve the practice of management – which often include requirements for associated improvements in leadership thinking and practice. These include total quality management, management by walking around, management by objectives, empowerment, matrix management, business process reengineering, knowledge management, core competencies, emotional intelligence, 360-degree feedback, authentic leadership, transformational leadership, six sigma, Lean manufacturing, Lean management, Lean six sigma, Lean strategy, agile, and other alchemical formulations that will soon take their place.

To varying degrees, these are all good ideas based upon the tangible existence of major problems in organizations of all sizes and types. Each of these programs, initiatives, processes, and systems invariably come under criticism within a few years after their introduction into the marketplace of ideas. While some are conceptually simple, others are more elaborate. Some are easy to implement, others are difficult. The common characteristic that they all share is that they fall below promises or expectations – yet success is often declared by top leaders because success can be defined however they wish. Soon enough, it is either forgotten and people move on, or some remnants remain, most often in the form of tools, processes, or methods that are incorporated into the company's problem-solving toolbox – a toolbox whose expected or required users are workers, not leaders.

Organizations spend a lot of time and money on these efforts, often years in duration. But invariably, they either fail or fall into disuse. Many people offer thoughts on why things did not work out, but these are nearly always surface-level causes. There is little effort to identify the deeper causes of the shortcomings or failures (which this book hopes to correct!). Doing so is seen as a waste of time and effort, if not irrelevant, and likely embarrassing. It is clear from the earlier pages that these programs, initiatives, processes, and systems enter into the simple, ordered negentropic system that sooner or later negates them in whole or part. Not only are most leaders not interested in new ways of leading people, they have even less interest in completely replacing the current management system with a new one.

This is not a new problem. It goes back a century, and surely much longer than that. Professor Samuel Haber perhaps said it best when explaining why leaders in the early 20th century had little interest in the then-new, progressive Scientific Management [7]:

> "The very notion of a completely integrated, scientific system for the factory was a distraction [to businessmen]. The truly 'scientific' standard for 'an

honest day's work'... could not be established and maintained unless the entire factory was systematized. Yet most business firms, as Taylor himself once noted, need only be more efficient than their competitors. This was one of the reasons that businessmen preferred efficiency stunts, devices, and mechanisms to a complete system of scientific management. The adoption of a complete system was often not the most profitable use of investment capital. Here... commercial efficiency did not automatically come first. The system should be adopted, Taylor's most orthodox disciples asserted, even when it might not be a paying investment."

Thorstein Veblen, an insightful analyst of late 19th and early 20th century business and its leaders, put it more bluntly [8]:

"It is the testimony of these efficiency engineers that relatively few pecuniary captains in command of industrial enterprises have a sufficient comprehension of the technological facts to understand and accept the findings of the technological experts who so argue for the elimination of preventable wastes, even when the issue is presented statistically in terms of price... That the business community is so permeated with incapacity and lack of insight in technological matters is doubtless due proximately to the fact that their attention is habitually directed to the pecuniary issue of industrial enterprise... Coincidently, because they do not lend themselves to this facile rating [price], facts that will not admit of a quantitative statement and statistical handling [accounting] decline in men's esteem, considered as facts, and tend in some degree to lose the cogency which belongs to empirical reality. They may even come to be discounted as being of a lower order of reality, or may even be denied factual value."

Nothing has changed with respect to the three points Veblen raised. This illustrates the high degree of order, and in this case simplicity, that characterizes negentropic systems.

The types of changes that leadership and management improvement programs call for require levels of workmanship and workmanlike diligence for *governance* – meaning, other-regarding knowledge and skills – that most leaders do not possess because they lack the development of such skills in the process of their ascension to the highest levels of the organization. In a different world, such skills development would take place at the start of one's career and continue even after they reached the top [9].

There can also be a lack of desire. From leaders' perspective, new leadership and management improvement programs present them with another problem on top of the myriad other problems they must contend with every day [10]. Leaders also have to respond to social and business pressure and do what one's peers or competitors are doing. And because the true nature of these programs is unknown until you try it out for yourself, leaders allocate resources to introduce the change to the organization hoping to gain some modicum of useful benefit. However, leaders being conservative and highly attuned to the wide-ranging benefits of the status quo, will see to it, consciously or not, that changes are skillfully circumscribed in ways that do not affect the Institution of Leadership and the System of Profound Privilege. These new disordered entropic programs and related trainings – past, present, and future – seek to penetrate the ordered negentropic system. It will be absorbed and negated in whole or part. What does survive will be made to fit in the ordered negentropic system such that it is rendered benign.

All of this is much to the chagrin of those employees who seek improved leadership and management of the organization. They perpetually hope for better, as does each new generation of workers. However, the Institution of Leadership and the System of Profound Privilege is always in the negentropic forming stage, always adjusting to the external environment to maintain its authority. Despite the volume of intrusions of disordered entropic programs and related trainings, it does not transition to an entropic growth stage which would eventually cause it to die.

CHAPTER SUMMARY

To engage you, the reader, and improve your learning and retention, write a short narrative summarizing Chapter 2.

THINK

- How many bosses have you had whose thinking and actions were divergent from other leaders in the organization? Why were they divergent? What drove them to be that way? Did you like that kind of boss? Why or why not?

THINK

- Given the rigid constraints of the Institution of Leadership and System of Profound Privilege, how can the governance of organizations be improved?

Notes

[1] Rudolf Clausius coined the word "entropy." See https://en.wikipedia.org/wiki/Rudolf_Clausius. Also see https://en.wikipedia.org/wiki/Entropy, accessed 20 January 2023

[2] Learn the origins of the *portmanteau*, see https://en.wikipedia.org/wiki/Negentropy, accessed 20 January 2023

[3] Kuibar, V. (2009), "Survival of Civilization Through the Negentropic Form of Existence," *Journal of Siberian Federal University: Humanities and Social Sciences*, Volume 3, pp. 116-124

[4] One's work in service to the Institution of Leadership and the system of profound privilege is more honorable than giving in to other-regarding demands, presiding over failed products or programs, bankruptcy, or losing one's job.

[5] Snowden, D. and Boone, M. (2007), "A Leader's Framework for Decision-Making," *Harvard Business Review*, Volume 85, November, pp. 69-76

[6] All definitions of leadership can function as definitions of both good and bad leadership. If the definitions can mean any type of leadership, then the definitions mean nothing. See University of Exeter, Centre for Leadership Studies, (2009), "Leadership Definitions," https://web.archive.org/web/20090310035842/http://www.leadership-studies.com, 10 March, accessed 22 January 2023 and Bogenschneider, B.

(2016), "Leadership Epistemology," *Creighton Journal of Interdisciplinary Leadership*, Volume 2, Number 2, November, pp. 24-37, https://files.eric.ed.gov/fulltext/EJ1152190.pdf, accessed 22 January 2023. To comprehend the full scope of confusion concerning leadership, see University of Cambridge, Institute for Sustainability Research (2017), "Global Definitions of Leadership and Theories of Leadership Development: Literature Review," https://www.cisl.cam.ac.uk/resources/sustainability-leaders hip/global-definitions-of-leadership, accessed 22 January 2023 and "Leadership," https://en.wikipedia.org/wiki/ Leadership, accessed 22 January 2023

[7] Haber, S. (1964), *Efficiency and Uplift: Scientific Management and the Progressive Era 1890-1920*, The University of Chicago Press, Chicago, Illinois, pp. 16-17

[8] Veblen, T. (1914), *The Instinct of Workmanship*, The Macmillan Company, New York New York, p. 223, 224, and 245

[9] Liker, J. (2020), *The Toyota Way: 14 Management Principles from the World's Greatest Manufacturer*, Second Edition, McGraw-Hill, New York, New York

[10] One can have some empathy for leaders in this regard. It is commonly said that "leadership is hard." Taken as true, it is then no surprise that leaders would want to put problems into the Clear domain whenever they can. This, however, changes the perception of leadership from error-free to error- and mistake-prone.

3

Leaders and Sense-Making

To better understand how the Institution of Leadership and the System of Profound Privilege function in real-world practice, we can turn to Cynefin (pronounced *kuh-nev-in*) [1]. Cynefin is a dynamic framework used for making sense of the context in which problems exist based on the relationship between cause-and-effect (Figure 3-1). It allows leaders to align decision-making with the type of problem that they face. The Cynefin framework consists of five domains: Clear and Complicated (ordered, predictable), Complex and Chaotic (unpredictable), and Aporetic/Confused [2]. Our focus will be the Clear domain – formerly labeled "Simple," and "Obvious" prior to that. All three characterizations are important in relation to the following analysis.

When leaders, particularly top leaders, face problems in any era of time or place, their predisposition is to simplify the problem. Whether the problem exists in the Complicated, Complex, or Chaotic domains, they think or desire the problem to be Clear; that the problem is ordered with a known or easily knowable cause-and-effect whose outcome is predictable. If they are wrong, as if often the case [3], then resulting decisions and actions will eventually lead to falling off the cliff and throwing the business (the system) into chaos [4] (see Introduction, Note 4, corporate calamities). It then becomes very expensive and time consuming for leaders and the rest of the organization to climb out of the cliff – meaning, to correct the problem. Such problems often drag on for years. In the Cynefin framework "falling off the cliff" is attributed to leader's complacency, which in Figure 3-1 straddles the Chaotic and Clear domains.

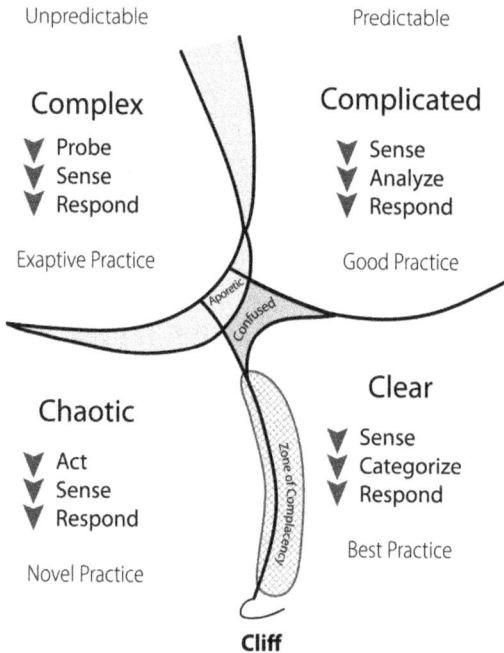

Figure 3-1. Cynefin framework. The cliff is denoted by the C-shaped line at the bottom of the boundary between Clear and Chaotic [1]. See Note 4 for a representation of the cliff in three dimensions.

Complacency is the apparent cause, but it is not the actual cause. This attribution is the result of mistaken causality – the assumption that the effect (falling off the cliff) is Clear with a known cause (complacency) [5]. But it is not that. It is instead the requirement that leaders to adhere to the meticulous workmanship and workmanlike diligence of the

Institution of Leadership and the System of Profound Privilege, as informed by the cascading systems of preconceptions shown in Figure 1-1 [6]. Thus, every problem should follow the sense-categorize-respond "best practice" sequence. "Best practice is, by definition, past practice" [7].

Consciously or not, leaders are predisposed to driving problems into the domain that best fits their status and is congruent with their vested interests and their rights and privileges. In short, having the answer to any problem properly lies in the Clear domain, and it makes no difference whether the answer is right or wrong. The Institution of Leadership and the System of Profound Privilege has rigid constraints that require leaders to put their problems into the Clear domain of the Cynefin framework. Thus, the Cynefin view that leaders miss and mislabel problems as Complicated or Complex is incorrect, as is the assumption that complacency is the causal factor leading to chaos.

Any major corporate problem is usually the result of many small problems percolating for a long time at all levels of the organization. People are fully aware that these problems exist and take personal risks to inform leaders at every level so as to avoid catastrophe – falling off the cliff. But leaders don't want to hear of problems because acknowledging the existence of problems results in a lowering of their status by showing them to be poor leaders and managers. Furthermore, problems interfere with their vested interests and their rights and privileges. Consequently, most organizations are reactive to problems, not proactive, giving leaders ample freedom to blame others. Often companies are well known by their customers for being excellent firefighters but extremely poor at avoiding problems to begin with.

Importantly, leaders do not just drive problems into the Clear domain and process it with automated machine-like precision. They have another "best practice" ("past practice") which is to purposefully drive problems into other domains – Complicated, Complex, and Chaotic. The purpose of doing this is more than simple obfuscation. It is to delay consideration, delay taking action, postpone decisions, avoid variances to budgets or metrics, or simply hope that future events overtake the need to do anything now. Ultimately, hoping that the problem will go away. This is why leaders tell subordinates:

- Get more information
- Do a detailed analysis
- That sounds too risky
- We don't have the people
- Write a report
- It's not the right time for that
- You need to get approval from...
- Start over, your assumptions are wrong
- So and so needs to review that
- We need a team to look at this
- We don't have time for that
- You need to do more experiments
- We need to hire a consultant
- Have so and so get involved
- This problem belongs to another group

- We'll put it in next year's budget
- We have to push out the meeting
- You need to gather more data

As a practical matter, leaders, with or without knowing it, cleverly use the Cynefin framework is a way that is not intended. They move problems to and from the five domains whenever it suits their interests, as is their right to do. The patterned arrows in Figure 3-2 depict the movement of problems in and out of the Clear, Complicated, Complex, Chaotic, and Aporetic/Confused domains. Creating complexity and chaos is beneficial to leaders as it justifies the need for strong leadership and allows leaders to exert power in workmanlike ways to get what they want. It also perpetuates the Institution of Leadership and the System of Profound Privilege, which applies more to self-regarding proclivities than other-regarding proclivities – i.e., *governance*. The "Zone of Complacency" is more like the "Zone of Self-Regarding Risk Reduction" entailing fine workmanship and workmanlike diligence. From this we can see why organizations suffer from both perpetual and recurring problems as well as periodic corporate calamities that require heroic rescue by top leaders.

Paradoxically, the rigid constraints of the Institution of Leadership and the System of Profound Privilege give leaders great flexibility, and it is therefore worth defending and preserving. Leaders are often characterized as being overconfident and lacking humility. This is no surprise when one considers their deft handling of any type of problem in any context. Everything consists of "known knowns" (Clear

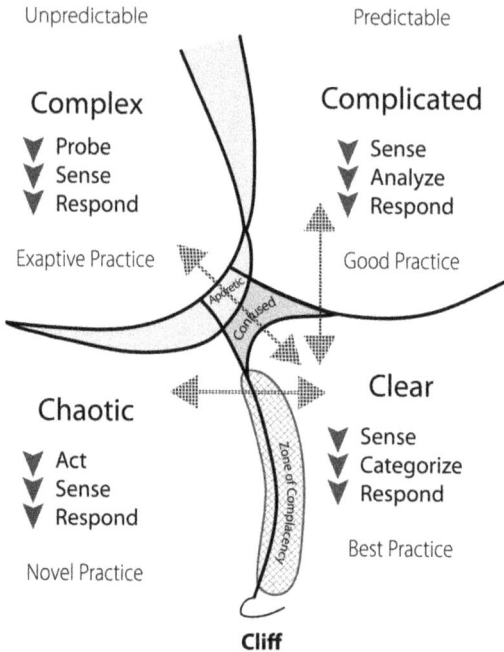

Figure 3-2. The patterned arrows depict the movement (throttling) of problems between different domains by leaders.

domain), as leaders dislike the other domains – unless they can be put to good use. "Known unknowns" (Complicated domain), "unknown unknowns" (Complex domain), "unimagined unknowables" (Chaos domain) and "don't know" (Aporetic/Confused domain) can either magically be turned into "known knowns" or used to one's advantage – to cause a disturbance, control others, hide problems, defeat rivals, create problems, inject chaos, run out the clock, divert attention, camouflage incompetence, gain or maintain status, increase personal wealth, or justify a decision or course of action. The political nature of most organizations assures these domains will be manipulated, consciously or not, under the sanctified rigid constraints of the Institution of Leadership and the System of Profound Privilege.

Leader's may understand that business is complex, perhaps often chaotic and unpredictable, but that does not usually propel them to think of problems in contexts other than Clear domain. A simple example illustrates the point. When the biggest problems arise, leaders' "entrained thinking" (P-intelligence) expertly guides them to see a simple and obvious linear cause-and-effect: e.g., the cause of the problem is that someone lower in the hierarchy did not do their job. The sense-categorize-response sequence informs the boss that the problem is best corrected by blaming the person, micromanaging the person, or replacing the person. In the Clear domain it is assumed that leader and subordinates have access to the information needed to correct the situation. Yet many a person has been felled by presenting facts to leaders that they could easily access. Facts are not the point of interest. Factors such as power, status, vested interests, rights privileges, honor, and prestige are far more important. Understanding this leads to a different understanding of complexity – a different way of thinking about the world.

From prior experience accumulated over more than 170 generations, leaders know that they can take the chance – a much better than even chance – that things will work out in their favor. After all, they have legions of subordinates to fix the problems that they create, and they control budgets. They can allocate the millions or billions that are needed to correct the problems. If the problems are so severe as to cost them their job, they will be reemployed soon enough, perhaps at a higher level, or become self-employed as a private equity investor or consultant. Interestingly, leaders' headlong rush into artificial intelligence and advanced automated machinery will soon leave them with far fewer employees to blame and fix problems (but more suppliers), and many may become more exposed to being seen as incompetent. Leaders might then have to start using the Cynefin framework as it is intended or think of a workaround that preserves and perpetuates the Institution of Leadership and the System of Profound Privilege. Machines know nothing about CXO status, power, vested interests, rights, privileges or honor. Only people do – for now.

In the meantime, the leader's framework for decision-making remains as shown in Figures 3-3 [8] and 3-4.

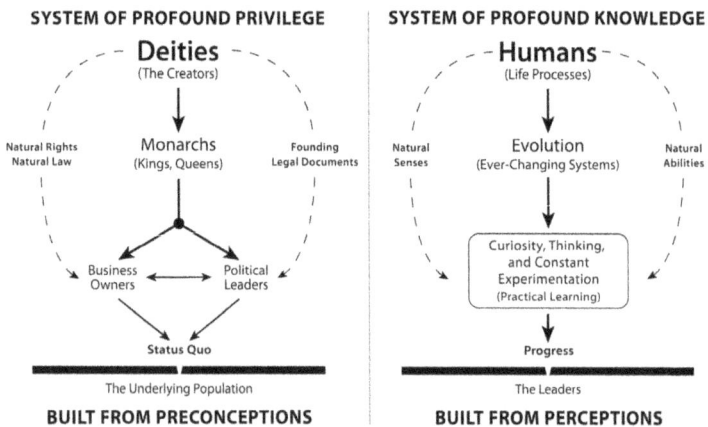

SYSTEM OF PROFOUND PRIVILEGE	SYSTEM OF PROFOUND KNOWLEDGE
Deities (The Creators)	**Humans** (Life Processes)
Natural Rights / Natural Law — Monarchs (Kings, Queens) — Founding Legal Documents	Natural Senses — Evolution (Ever-Changing Systems) — Natural Abilities
Business Owners ← → Political Leaders	Curiosity, Thinking, and Constant Experimentation (Practical Learning)
Status Quo	Progress
The Underlying Population	The Leaders
BUILT FROM PRECONCEPTIONS	**BUILT FROM PERCEPTIONS**

Figure 3-3. The System of Profound Privilege (SoPP, left) compared to a conceptualization of W. Edwards Deming's System of Profound Knowledge (SoPK, right). See Note 8 for descriptions of the Institution of Leadership and the System of Profound Privilege.

In Figure 3-3, the top of the System of Profound Privilege (SoPP) diagram denotes the starting point for the Human Supersystem of Preconceptions (HSP) that informs the Organizational Macrosystem of Preconceptions (OMP) that informs the Individual Microsystem of Preconceptions (IMP) that guides leader's day-to-day and strategic thinking and actions. This contrasts vividly with W. Edward Deming's System of Profound Knowledge (SoPP) [9], which, from most leaders' viewpoint for the last 25 years is irrelevant because it is messy and cognitively obtrusive (i.e., facts are often inconvenient for leaders, not just for the past 25 years but for thousands of years). Changing preconceptions from SoPP to SoPK violates the established rigid constraints of the Institution of Leadership [10] and is attempted by only a few. If successful, their epiphany and subsequent workmanship are soon reversed upon changes in leadership.

Figure 3-4 places the SoPP and SoPK images in the associated Cynefin framework domains. SoPP is in the Clear domain while SoPK is in the Complicated, Complex, and Chaotic domain. The latter three domains are where problem-solving follows the approach of "analyze good practice," "probe emergent practice," and "act with novel practice," respectively [7]. These problem-solving approaches are consistent with the approaches to scientific problem-solving rooted in sensory perceptions advocated by W. Edwards Deming and many others, in contrast to the non-scientific approach to problem-solving used by most leaders that is rooted in SoPP preconceptions.

However, from the perspective of most top leaders, there are

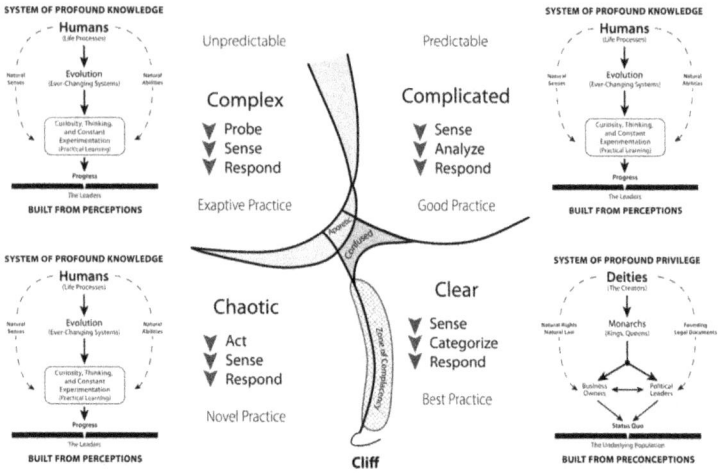

Figure 3-4. The System of Profound Privilege and the System of Profound Knowledge diagrams placed adjacent to the corresponding Cynefin domains.

some practical limitations to contextualizing problems [1, 7]. For problems in the Complicated domain, leaders are advised to follow "good practice," i.e., speak to experts and consider different options. Often, leaders ignore the advice of experts and the option chosen is the one consistent with past practices due to path dependence (i.e., Clear domain). For problems in the Complex domain, leaders are advised to follow "exaptive practice;" i.e., repurpose something intended to address one thing and use it for a different thing. In most cases, repurposing comes with a loss in fidelity of the original thing or a degradation in understanding or use that limits its effectiveness. This may involve experiments. However, most leaders are risk-averse and dislike experimenting, as well as the detailed structure required to achieve useful results (good or bad). For problems in the Chaotic domain, leaders are advised to follow "novel practice;" i.e., create something different from what is known or exists. Most leaders look for solutions to problems external to the organization. Often, that is because they have little faith in the knowledge and creativity of employees and fail to understand how they themselves create that situation. So, they look for solutions that they can simply purchase from suppliers.

The contextualization of problems in this way provides additional insight as to why most leaders drive problems into the domain that best fits with their status and is congruent with their vested interests and their rights and privileges – the Clear domain [10]. Leaders' sense-making context, most often, is *rex primus est* [11-13].

CHAPTER SUMMARY

To engage you, the reader, and improve your learning and retention, write a short narrative summarizing Chapter 3.

THINK

- Identify examples where leaders moved an important problem from the Complicated, Complex, or Chaotic domains to the Clear domain.

- Identify recurring problems in your workplace.

THINK

- "Best practice is, by definition, past practice" What practices in your organization best fit this statement?

- What problems have leaders been warned about in your organization – problems that later turned into much bigger problems?

THINK

- Identify problems in the Clear domain that the leaders of your organization have moved into the Complicated, Complex, or Chaotic domain.

- Speculate as to the epoch in time when leadership shifted from being other-regarding to self-regarding. See https://en.wikipedia.org/wiki/List_of_time_periods

Notes

[1] Snowden, D. and Friends (2022), *Cynefin: Weaving Sense-Making into the Fabric of Our World*, Second Edition, Cognitive Edge Ltd., The Cynefin Company. Cynefin® is a registered trademark of Cognitive Edge Ltd. Cynefin means "habitat" in Welsh. See also https://cynefin.io/wiki/Main_Page

[2] Cynefin definitions: "Exaptive: The taking of an idea, concept, tool, method, framework, etc., intended to address one thing, and using it to address a different thing, often in another domain." "Novel: Different from anything known or existing before, possibly resulting from exaptation." "Aporetic: …the epistemological state of not having made sense of a given context, while being aware of such ignorance and having an intentional attitude towards overcoming it. Also, the liminal portion of the 'confused' domain." "Confused: …a state of not knowing the type of decision domain being faced, while not necessarily being aware of that." Source: https://cynefin.io/wiki/Glossary, accessed 22 January 2023

[3] Emiliani, B. and Torinesi, M. (2021), *Wheel of Fortune: Getting to the Heart of Business Strategy*, Cubic LLC, South Kingstown, Rhode Island

[4] To view a three-dimensional image of the Cynefin framework, and to better visualize and understand the cliff, see https://www.vige.se/blog/2020/6/20/cynefinvige as well as https://thecynefin.co/cynefin-st-davids-day-2019-3-of-5/, accessed 22 January 2023

[5] Unfortunately, this throws the Cynefin framework into a bit of chaos.

[6] Emiliani, B. (2022), *A Changed Perspective: An Essential Guide for Emerging Leaders*, Cubic LLC, South Kingstown, Rhode Island

[7] Snowden, D. and Boone, M. (2007), "A Leader's Framework for Decision-Making," *Harvard Business Review*, Volume 85, November, pp. 69-76

[8] Emiliani, B. (2020), *Irrational Institutions: Business, Its Leaders, and The Lean Movement*, Cubic LLC, South Kingstown, Rhode Island

[9] Deming, W. (1994), *The New Economics: For Industry, Government, Education*, Second Edition, Chapter 4, The W. Edwards Deming Institute, Ketchum, Idaho

[10] In the busy, pressure-filled real-world settings, most leaders are not likely to process (contextualize) their many difficult problems through the Cynefin framework. Expediency reigns. This is not just due to the habit of driving problems into the Clear domain. Expediency is tradition ("best practice") in the Institution of Leadership and the System of Profound Privilege to do so. Furthermore, most people have great difficulty doing formal root cause analysis well. These methods are seen by leaders as useful tools for people at lower levels of the organization to solve their work-related problems and who have time for such investigations. Having given formal root cause analysis homework

assignments to working professional students for over 15 years, their native abilities to perform such analyses are poor and get better only through diligent daily or weekly practice. Additionally, a few hundred of these graduate students were asked if they have ever seen a formal root cause analysis performed by an executive (general manager or higher). An affirmative answer came from only two students (one general manager and one vice president). The higher one's status, the less likely they are to use structured problem-solving tools. And should they (or subordinates) do so, they always reserve the right to ignore the result and the specified corrective actions. Leaders rarely have complete and accurate information about problems – not because such a thing is impossible to achieve, but because people are afraid to tell the boss the truth. And leaders usually assume that the information (narrative) or analysis provided to them is free of other forms of bias, the various forms of illogical thinking, or personal or political agendas. This leads to inaccurate or wrong causal analyses and subsequent decision-making, often precipitating the previously mentioned corporate calamities.

[11] It is also important to make the link between corporate calamities and the cognitive biases and illogical thinking that permeates leadership thinking and decision-making. These also pay a significant role in leaders' efforts to drive major problems to the Clear domain. For an accounting of this, across scores of corporate calamities, see Note 3, Figures 3-1 and 3-2 (pages 75-78).

[12] In the minds of most top leaders, there is an exact or near equivalency between the I-frame and Clear domain,

while the S-frame is seen as something different than any of the other domains – thus, a sixth domain, "Closed;" i.e., cut off from, to shut, block, or make inaccessible. The sequence is "sense-categorize-divert" is a domain of "No Practice" where problem-solving is sensed as either objectionable or impossible (Figure 3-5). This intensifies the spiritual belief in I-frame solutions to most or all problems.

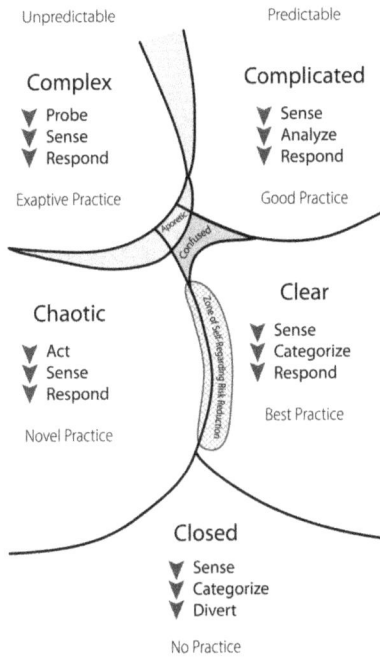

Figure 3-5. Cynefin+1 framework. The cliff between the Chaotic and Clear domain is eliminated because it is inconsequential to the Institution of Leadership and the System of Profound Privilege. The sixth domain, Closed, is a domain of sense-making where problem-solving is not allowed. Hence, "No Practice." The sequence sense-categorize-divert redirects sense-making towards the pragmatic utility and consistent benefits of the Clear domain. Closed is a Gordian constrained SoPP-affiliated domain.

[13] If one were to create an image of the Institution of Leadership, it could be best depicted as a fractal in the shape of a 3-dimensional logarithmic spiral, as shown in Figure 3-6. German printmaker Albrecht Dürer (1471-1528) called the logarithmic spiral the "eternal line" – in our case, an eternal lineage connecting leaders across time and space to possess the same or similar social habits of thought and action; the passing along of traditions from one generation of leader to the next for 5,000 years or more. This will continue for the calculable future.

Figure 3-6. Depiction of the Institution of Leadership as a logarithmic fractal spiral representing an eternal lineage connecting leaders across time and space to possess the same or similar social habits of thought and action. The point of origin in the image is the epoch in time when leadership shifted from being other-regarding (S-frame) to self-regarding (I-frame) leading to the formation of the Institution of Leadership and the System of Profound Privilege.

4

Information Processing

Thus far we have discussed the cascade of preconceptions from the supersystem, through organizations, and to the individual, preconception-based intelligence (P-intelligence), fact-based intelligence (F-intelligence), frameworks for systems (S-frame) and individual frameworks (I-frame), negentropy, and the Cynefin sense-making framework. Together, these illuminate the contextual domains in which leaders understand problems. This understanding biases information processing and decision-making towards resolving spiritual anxieties – conflicts between social values and facts, and between moral judgments and scientific analysis. These conflicts, which favor preserving the Institution of Leadership and the System of Profound Privilege, necessarily must exclude relevant information from information processing and decision-making.

The chasm between the spiritual goals of leaders and the material work and material needs of workers is produced by cultural training requiring information to be processed such that it achieves leaders' spiritual, metaphysical, and material ends [1]. All other problems are reduced to "white noise" – problems emanating from the shop and office floors, employees, suppliers, and customers – and most often attended to by top leaders only in times of reduced financial performance, severe quality or delivery problems, or corporate calamity. Maintaining the S-frame of the Institution of Leadership and the System of Profound

Privilege requires the shifting of problems to I-frames. In doing so it denies the existence of interdependence between people, groups, organizations, and processes to produce economically desirable outcomes. The I-frame is strengthened by using metaphysical representations of individual and group performance: metrics, KPIs, spreadsheets, and dashboards. The numbers orientation, long part of leadership culture, is transferred down the hierarchy to sustain the popular preconception that "numbers don't lie." This works to the advantage of The Institution of Leadership and the System of Profound Privilege, as it conditions people to accept as necessary outcomes that are contrary to the interests of workers and society (e.g., layoffs).

The other-regarding knowledge and skills of governance are problematic to top leaders because they require fundamental shifts in wealth and power. The instinct of leaders' workmanship is to protect the house, not share it with others lower in the hierarchy [2, 3]. Information processing therefore must be weighted towards P-intelligence, inclusive of spiritual desires, myths, illusions, traditions, stories, and metaphysical signs and symbols. In contrast, the other-regarding knowledge and skills for governance are weighted towards F-intelligence (Figure 4-1), which, in corollary, is more contributive to the stability and advancement of society.

P-intelligence carries with it a glossy view of abundance which in turn drives competitive behaviors that produce conflict and exploitation. The associated information processing is along the lines of competitive gain, removed by

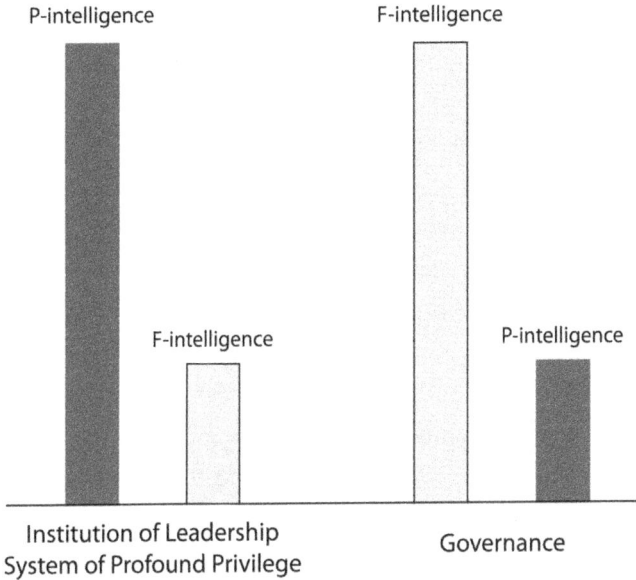

Figure 4-1. Relative weightings of P-intelligence and F-intelligence for the Institution of Leadership and the System of Profound Privilege compared to Governance of organizations (i.e., other-regarding knowledge and skills).

some distance from contact with facts of the material world. Human relationships constructed in terms of dominance and subservience for the primary purpose of spiritual satisfaction necessarily cancels or restricts any changes in information processing routines. Consequently, times arise now and then where top leaders become apprehensive that they have given away too much to workers in terms of pay, benefits, or perquisites, and believe that a correction is needed. This can be isolated to a specific organization or a become torrent among organizations in a particular industry or across industries. Leaders' sentiments change when their spiritual satisfaction begins to weaken, resulting in changes favorable to leaders that are often obfuscated by false narratives (e.g., stories of business hardship). This, predictably, has negative effects on the workforce in terms of engagement, commitment, and productivity.

The rise to the top of an organization progressively renders most leaders technically obsolete and incurious [4], which creates deficits in comprehension of the work that employees do. Business processes become abstractions leading to an idealized understanding of activities. The persistent complaint about worker productivity by both leaders and external analysts is repeatedly attributed to factors other than the dominance of P-intelligence and consistent efforts to place S-frame business problems into I-frames. With respect to the Cynefin framework, the productivity problem is predictably seen to lie in the Clear domain (i.e., "it's the workers' fault"). This domain becomes more relevant as one rises to higher levels in an organization. The sense-categorize-respond sequence becomes ever more highly developed and the "sense," "categorize," and "respond" elements each become more focused and consequential. This is consistent with the empirical observation that leaders perceive most problems to lie in the Clear domain.

Top leaders, being very influential, train their subordinates in this rigid response to problem-solving, who in turn train their subordinates down to the level of supervisor and worker [5]. This social learning process is akin to lightning tendrils that touch every leader in the organization. When lightning strikes, the boss' problem (or concern) quickly travels to those below who snap into action and apply the speedy sense-categorize-respond sequence. Impatient leaders are not generally known to be advocates of sense-analyze-respond (Complicated domain) or probe-sense-respond (Complex domain) because "analyze" and "probe" are seen as temporally inconsistent with taking fast action – unless their aim is subterfuge or sabotage. Generally, they want answers now. Those who excel at working in the Clear domain – the domain that best satisfies leaders' interests – and who accept traditions and myths and view them as aspirational, are typically seen as good candidates for promotion to executive levels and as accreditable conveyors of ancient traditions to future generations.

Top business leaders do not just have influence internally in the organization, but externally as well. If a top leader of a publicly traded company is worried about something and takes action, then other leaders in companies large and small will notice and likely follow that action because they assume the influential leader knows something that they do not know. One's reputation as a titan of industry sets into motion a large-scale sense-categorize-respond sequence among top leaders within an industry or between industries. For example, an increase in interest rates and a slowdown in economic growth triggers widespread layoffs (diminution in human welfare) even when unemployment is low and the organization remains profitable. One leader copies another into the Clear domain, not just because it is expedient to do so. It is also because P-intelligence overrides F-intelligence and S-frame problems are shifted to become I-frame problems, all of which accrues to the survival of the negentropic Institution of Leadership and the System of

Profound Privilege. This happens in normal times as well as in times of crisis. Based on what top leaders say, the cause of layoffs appears to be economic. Its actual cause is political. But those laid off, and the public in general, believe what influential top leaders say: "The economy is weakening and so layoff are necessary." Recessions are normally thought to be caused entirely by economic slowdowns (reduction in aggregate demand). Instead, they should be seen as caused by a sudden acceleration of political interests (i.e., spiritual desires and fears), tightly coupled to a decline in economic activity depending upon the circumstances [6]. This is as close to supernatural power (i.e., controlling the distribution of wealth) as can be had by any human.

The periodic political imperative to muscularly exercise the Institution of Leadership (social habits of thought and action) and the System of Profound Privilege (the vested rights and interests that leaders protect and preserve) is achieved by throwing employees off the cliff and into financial and emotional chaos. In this way, society makes its contribution to preserving and perpetuating the Institution of Leadership and the System of Profound Privilege. The workmanship of leaders is to process information such that decisions are made that inflict chronic stress on those lower in the Natural Social Order, most often in the forms of a constant demands for greater productivity, constant fear of job loss, or both [7]. Workers are taken for rides that they do not want to be on – often psychologically barbaric rides of that negatively impact their lives and livelihoods. Keeping the Institution of Leadership and the System of Profound Privilege stable over time generates instabilities in people lives, society, the macroeconomic system, and government.

The rights, privileges, and obligations of the Institution of Leadership and the System of Profound Privilege demand that it be ever-present in the minds of top leaders. It deeply colors their thinking and rigidly constrains them, whether they realize it or not, because it is fixed into the common sense of the community of top leaders. For example, a top leader will occasionally seek advice from other top leaders. They might ask the same question to five of their peers. Four will provide answers that lie within the status quo – common solutions to problems listed in the CEO playbook – while one does not. There is a high likelihood that the outlier's advice, no matter how cogent it is, will be ignored [8] in favor of the four answers that are consistent with longstanding traditions and preconceptions.

A great confidence comes from being among the few persons charged with carrying forward revered ancient traditions. The process is nearly irreversible in the sense of becoming more other-regarding than self-regarding and in making a transition from I-frame to S-frame problem-solving. Exposure to facts do not matter anymore. The leadership in-group has its own version of truth that can be nearly impossible to penetrate. Many people have presented facts leading to obvious courses of action only to see the top leader ignore the facts and order a different course of action, one that is often at odds with prior statements or decisions. People are led to believe that the goals of business are simple and expressed simply as profits and share price, cash flow and customer satisfaction, the creation and delivery of products and services, but there is much more going on than just that [9].

An important aspect of leadership is to shape and align people's preconceptions to the Institution of Leadership and the System of Profound Privilege. Doing so reduces resistance to the types of changes that favor leaders' interests. For example, a top leader says that a new technology such as OpenAI's ChatGPT chatbot will increase human productivity, which in turn would increase economic growth and raise wages. Is that true? It depends. Increases in productivity, growth, wages are potential benefits, not necessarily actual benefits. Higher productivity often leads to layoffs, and economic growth benefits those at the top of the Natural Social Order more than those at the bottom. Wages will increase only to the extent that top leaders are willing to share in the gains of productivity and economic growth. The approach to setting wages over the last 40-plus years has been market-based, not based on productivity or economic growth. Furthermore, machines that contribute to creating labor surplus, such as AI will likely do, helps leaders by putting constant downward pressure on wages. And it also helps them avoid direct responsibility for immiseration and any related social and political problems [10].

In the recent past, top leaders were fond of the slogan "maximize shareholder value," implying that efforts to achieve such an outcome benefitted the whole of society. It did not [11]. Leaders say a lot of things to get people lower in the Natural Social Order to believe that benefits will somehow accrue to them, when the benefits, or largest share of benefits, in fact accrue to others. In sum, leaders process information in ways that make the most sense to them in relation to their social status and job responsibilities. People at lower levels do the same. But what is peculiar about top leaders is the requirement to manage their vested interests in sustaining and perpetuating the Institution of Leadership and the System of Profound Privilege as well as the work of governance (other-regarding knowledge and skills). Historically, the balance has always been tilted strongly in favor of the Institution of Leadership and the System of Profound Privilege, interspersed with brief periods where interests between that and governance have been better balanced. Better balance is important because prolonged imbalances lead to great social and political upheavals that one would be wise to avoid [12-14]. Leaders do not have a Natural Right to impoverish people or make their lives more difficult than necessary. Economics is not zero-sum, but it usually is in practice, driven by competitive forces that glorify individual success.

The hope for changes in the status quo is often affixed to generational change. There may be some merit in that, but it is less than one might imagine [15]. Every 30 years or so, a new generation begins to replace the older generation. However, the younger generation is always greatly influenced by older generations. The younger generation may view some things differently, but the teachings of older generations are deeply embedded and will emerge sooner or later. The marginal benefits gained from supporting long-established systems, rather than opposing them, likewise will be seen, sooner or later, as more attractive. It attests to the fine workmanship and workmanlike diligence directed towards preserving the Institution of Leadership and the System of Profound Privilege since ancient times [16].

CHAPTER SUMMARY

To engage you, the reader, and improve your learning and retention, write a short narrative summarizing Chapter 4.

THINK

- Estimate the ratio of P-intelligence to F-intelligence as a function of the Natural Social Order.

Natural Social Order	P-F Ratio
Monarchs	
Business Leaders	
Politicians	
Society	
Groups	
Individuals	
Customers	
Suppliers	
Labor Unions	
Salaried Labor	
Hourly Labor	
Poor	
Indolent	

THINK

- You process information in ways that makes the most sense to you in relation to your social status and job responsibilities. Identify some social status and job factors that make you think the way you do.

THINK

- List the marginal benefits that you gain from supporting the Institution of Leadership and the System of Profound Privilege.

Notes

[1] Spiritual ends include status, prestige, honor, success, money, and its materialistic manifestations – the accumulation of physical property.

[2] It seems top leaders lose their instinct for the workmanship of governance because their survival is not immediately at stake in the same way that it is for workers.

[3] The dichotomy between the workmanship and workmanlike diligence of preserving the Institution of Leadership and System of Profound Privilege and the work of governance also exists in the realm of elected politicians.

[4] Leaders remain very curious about the traditional ways of thinking and doing things, but they are mostly incurious about new ways of thinking and doing things. In a very real sense, this becomes a straightjacket for both the leaders and the led. Consequently, change and progress are delimited.

[5] Coming under the tutelage of one's elders via mentoring or coaching is both flattering and seen as beneficial by the underling. But it is, in the main, a conditioning of the underling to take on certain points of view rooted in the traditions and myths of the past (P-intelligence) with the intent to perpetuate them, knowingly or not. The training is directed towards the acceptance of precedents favored by the older generations.

[6] This encompasses the whole of business cycles.

[7] An example of this pertains the United States, where income taxes on those highest in the Natural Social Order have been dramatically reduced over recent decades. That, coupled with large business bailouts and banking system rescues have produced large budget deficits. Politicians' solution is to turn this S-frame problem into an I-frame problem of cutting earned and unearned benefits to those lowest in the Natural Social Order; to compel them onto a path of self-reliance regardless of if that is possible. The actual solution to the S-frame problem is to raise taxes on those with the highest incomes and allow businesses and banks to recognize and contend with their risks. But that solution has been out of reach because it negatively impinges upon the Institution of Leadership and the System of Profound Privilege and the associated economic, social, and political outcomes that foster its preservation. The result is increased debt due to continued borrowing and interest payments. This undercuts the abilities of those lowest in the Natural Social Order to live long healthy and productive lives, and it leads to reductions in birth rates and lower economic growth. Wealthy opponents of tax increases proffer spiritual-based arguments, and often false arguments as well, rather than evidence-based arguments to maintain the status quo. Because they are influential, people lower in the Natural Social Order believe them, much to their own (continuing) disadvantage.

[8] The need to preserve and perpetuate the Institution of Leadership and the System of Profound Privilege explains why most efforts to "transform" organizations, leadership, or management practice has a dismal record of success.

Transformation, if called for by the top leader, usually means to purchase solutions to their problems from suppliers, thus delegating workmanship and workmanlike diligence to them. This is often necessary. Other times it is a substitute for leaders applying their own workmanship and workmanlike diligence to problems and setting the good example for others to follow – the examples that are often talked about but which few do.

[9] Some readers might construe such a statement, or this book, to suggest the existence of conspiracy. There is no such activity going on. Instead, it is merely the common sense of a class a people doing their job in a largely uncoordinated fashion. The social behavior and norms (culture) of leadership obviously differs from the cultures of groups lower in the Natural Social Order.

[10] According to Microsoft co-founder and former CEO Bill Gates, "This will change the world... We find ourselves with a tool that can make even white collar type jobs far more efficient... Reading and writing are now within A.I.'s capabilities and that will have a very broad impact... The progress over the next couple of years to make these things even better will be profound." Bove, T. (2023), "Bill Gates says ChatGPT will 'change our world' but it doesn't mean your job is at risk," *Fortune*, 10 February, https://fortune .com/2023/02/10/bill-gates-chatgpt-jobs-chatbot-microsof t-google-bard-bing/, accessed 10 February 2023. ChatGPT dutifully parrots the perspective of most top leaders, saying that "...while some tasks may be automated, technology like me can also help to augment and support human workers,

enabling them to be more productive and efficient in their roles... It is important to note that while some jobs may be lost due to A.I., new job opportunities are also likely to be created as businesses and organizations adopt and make use of these new technologies. The key challenge will be to ensure that workers have the skills and training needed to transition into these new job opportunities." Pringle, E. (2023), "We asked ChatGPT which jobs it thinks it will replace – and it's not good news for data entry professionals or reporters," *Fortune*, 8 February, https://fortune.com/2023 /02/08/we-asked-chatgpt-jobs-it-will-replace-openai-data-p rocessing-customer-service/, accessed 11 February 2023. AI's presumed "authority" will readily feed people's confirmation biases. The "skills and training" that workers will need to successfully transition to new jobs (many surely at lower pay) will likely be positioned as an I-frame problem for job seekers and also cast out onto the I-frame of public education – the long-maligned K-12, vocational, and higher education teachers – thereby allowing corporations to evade responsibility for their adoption of job-changing, job-killing, and wage depressing AI technologies. The hope is that AI will create new industries and demand for new types of jobs. It will no doubt do that. But this leads to important questions that economists, politicians, policymakers, and business leaders, perpetually enthusiastic about new technologies and the anticipated gains in productivity, profits, and gross domestic product, typically do not thoroughly consider and which can lead to family distress and social unrest: Will the addition of new jobs exceed the displacement of old jobs? What is the *rate* at which the old jobs be displaced? Will it be faster than the rate at which they can be replaced? And will the resulting pay be lower or higher? Additionally, retraining displaced workers always proceeds at a slower pace than the pace of technology development, consistently rendering retraining less useful than planned. The expected outcome should be lower demand for labor, lower wages, and concomitant family distress and social unrest. It seems wise that economists, politicians, policymakers, and business leaders should plan for these being the most likely outcomes (which, economists, politicians, policymakers being endlessly optimistic and anchored in archaic preconceptions, famously did not consider in their pious promotion of offshoring work to low-wage countries in the years 1990-2019, and who now admit it was a grave error). If AI does not result in lower demand for labor and concomitant family distress and social unrest, then great! These leaders will have wisely planned for the worse and achieved better than expected outcomes, and faith in them will be restored (at least for a couple of generations, after which such wisdom will be likely be forgotten).

[11] In the United States, this coincided with some two decades of offshoring work and the financialization of business, resulting in millions of lost jobs and depressed wages, impacting tens of millions of people.

[12] Turchin, P. and Nefedov, S. (2009), *Secular Cycles*, Princeton University Press, Princeton, New Jersey

[13] Acemoglu D. and Robinson, J. (2012), *Why Nations Fail: The Origins of Power, Prosperity, and Poverty*, Crown Publishers, New York, New York

[14] Paeans of greatness, whether in the context of company or nation, are dangerous. They constitute myths and stories that favor maintaining the status quo which will eventually lead to demise. The status quo, grounded in P-intelligence, is a type of information pathology that blocks and distorts information and confuses, obscures, or negates facts. This inevitably leads to organizational distress or failure. Consequently, the status quo is clearly seen as illogical to those grounded in F-intelligence. There is a need to evolve continuously and judiciously determine, periodically, which traditions must be kept, and which must be modified or abandoned to allow for needed adjustments that are beneficial to all of humanity.

[15] Gaining widespread acceptance for the I-frame, whether in society or a company, discourages the formation of groups that could upset the status quo (or assures that groups remain small and ineffectual).

[16] There is a general failure by society to comprehend the centuries of iterative efforts that have been applied to protect and preserve leaders' rights and privileges. These efforts are typically obscured by persistent ritualistic messaging of freedom and empowerment in the post-modern era (i.e., I-framing, whether in the context of private enterprise or society). See https://en.wikipedia.org/wiki/Modern_era

Closing Comments

A book like this, and the other books that I have written since 2018, invariably leaves readers longing for answers to questions. As you have no doubt surmised, this is an extremely difficult problem for which there is no easy answer (or Cynefin domain). Over time, the slow drift of change has led to substantial improvement in overall well-being of societies across the globe. Yet, there remains intolerable levels of poverty, oppression, and corruption. There is no guarantee that past trends will continue to produce future improvements. Socio-economic and political events tend to go in cycles. As memories of past problems or past successes fade, they are destined to be relived again in the same or similar ways. Solutions to pressing problems sometimes materialize as cycles start or end. Time will tell. However, it seems certain that the Institution of Leadership and the System of Profound Privilege will continue to exist and may even strengthen as societies change, as AI technology improves, or as the human habitat changes, inclusive of resource competition.

What is potentially more amenable to change, even if only temporarily, is the other-regarding knowledge and skills of governance. People are always working to try and do that, though their I-frame prescriptions are produced in the absence of a thorough understanding of the Institution of Leadership and the System of Profound Privilege. That is what the series of books listed on page v hopes to change. Simply put, legions of people need to know what they are up against if they expect to change systems, to better balance P-intelligence and F-intelligence, and to redirect many problems from the I-frame to the S-frame where they belong. Continuing such efforts in the absence of this knowledge forces people to rely on luck or the passing of time instead of F-intelligence and creativity.

The common refrain is that capitalism is to blame or that leaders fear change. The phenomena presented in this book predate capitalism. Top leaders don't fear *technological* change, but they do fear *social* change [1]. That is why leadership improvement training, methods, and programs are, in most cases, destined to fail. They are fundamentally weak because they are based on an incomplete or incorrect understanding of leaders and their purpose. Where they do succeed, reversal is almost a certainty when leaders or owners change – if not on the first round of change, then surely the second or third.

A common mistake made by people seeking to improve leadership is that they assume leaders want to improve and become better at providing for the wants and needs of others. Some genuinely do, but for most others it is merely performative displays of interest to avoid being perceived as belligerent or uncooperative. Still, leadership training and development remains big business. It is not the first industry to profitably exist while producing so little in the way of tangible results. Perhaps we rely too much on leaders and companies for things that they were never designed to deliver.

As people rise through the hierarchy, the more of a team player they must become to fit in with their social peer group.

In doing so they must, in some measure, surrender their ability to think independently and do what should be done to advance human interests as times and circumstances change. Increased power seems to be correlated to a reduction of intelligence in terms of critical thinking and the actions resulting from it. The outcome is continuity and control, and, remarkably enough, stability – until which time continuity, control, and stability are seen to have run their course. Leadership training courses, particularly those seeking to improve leadership behaviors, are ill-suited to developing the level of critical thinking that leaders should have to operate organizations more efficiently, effectively, and humanely.

What is unusual is the extent to which leaders are disinterested in understanding how they interfere with worker's jobs in ways that reduce their individual and collective quality of workmanship and productivity. High status assures such disinterest. So instead, leaders place their faith in machines and software to improve quality and productivity and ignore the basic interactions with employees that generate significant waste (money, time, and material resources), cause delays and rework [2] – as well as working on the wrong things to begin with. It is no surprise that workers get blamed for their failings, given that the shift from S-frame to I-frame proves so useful under an incredibly wide range of circumstances. The workmanship and workmanlike diligence applied to generating problems for workers highlights the need for changes in governance from self-regarding to other-regarding. While this can be achieved without diminishing leaders' rights and privileges, the fallacious "slippery slope" argument invoked by leaders quickly subverts any changes to the status quo. One obvious area for improvement that might do some good is to show leaders, from supervisor to CEO, how their beliefs and untested assumptions, cognitive biases, illogical thinking [3], P-intelligence [4], and I-framing seamlessly work their way into business processes and generate S-frame failures that can cause them big troubles [5]. Even if the Institution of Leadership and the System of Profound Privilege goes unchanged or strengthens its grip, at least the number and severity of problems can be reduced, and likely many problems prevented, thus having far less negative impact on the organization, workers, and society. Leaders will not relinquish power, privilege, and wealth. But their contribution to society, and business results, would be greater if they were less inclined to throw those lower in the Natural Social Order off the cliff [6]. It truly is the least that leaders can do for their fellow human beings – not fully out of the kindness of their hearts, but for better and more consistent business results.

This proposed new idea for improvement is yet another I-frame solution to an S-frame problem. Consequently, it may not be any more successful than the many other I-frame interventions used in recent decades. But what needs to be attempted is a more holistic combination of this type of rigorous I-frame intervention with S-frame interventions. Together they may have a greater potential produce a different kind of leadership, one that is better suited to successfully take on the challenges of current and future times [7, 8].

The aim of this book, as well as my earlier works (see page v), is to answer scores of questions about how leaders think, how they behave, and why they do what they do, down to levels far deeper and more detailed than other analyses. Feedback from readers suggests that I have been successful at achieving this in previous works, and hopefully with this book as well. The fact that easy solutions remain elusive illustrates how 50 centuries of fine workmanship and workmanlike diligence make the Institution of Leadership and the System of Profound Privilege seemingly impenetrable. Yet all systems have vulnerabilities. The question is, can vulnerabilities be found and exploited faster than they can be fortified?

• • • •

This book has given you some different ways to see things. It gives you much to think about and perhaps inspires you to develop new and innovative solutions to try. I wish you well in your efforts to rethink the common understanding and practice of leadership.

BOOK SUMMARY (1 of 2)

To engage you, the reader, and improve your learning and retention, write a short narrative summarizing this book.

BOOK SUMMARY (2 of 2)

To engage you, the reader, and improve your learning and retention, write a short narrative summarizing this book.

THINK

- Try to think of combinations of I-frame and S-frame interventions that have the potential to produce a different kind of leadership, one that is better suited to current and future times.

THINK (1 of 2)

- Based on what you learned in this book, what will you teach to others?

THINK (2 of 2)

- Based on what you learned in this book, what will you teach to others?

Notes

[1] What has been the great and enduring appeal of machine technology to top leaders over the centuries? Is there more to it than simply higher productivity, profits, enterprise value, and the like? Consider if a leader implicitly or explicitly views business as a war-like competition, then they will surely want to obtain the necessary machine technologies to win or to preserve their winning edge against perceived adversaries – i.e., other corporations, governments, labor, NGOs, society, etc. – and to assure they have as much freedom as they desire. Consequently, governance (other-regarding knowledge and skills) need only be good enough to avoid losing wars (e.g., social change), while conceding that some minor battles might be lost. Machine technologies could be seen by top leaders as a practical way to slow down or avert the kinds of social change that have the potential to disrupt the Institution of Leadership and the System of Profound Privilege. Leaders' devotion to machine technology may thus be motivated in part by deep-rooted socio-political and spiritual needs as much as economic needs.

[2] Emiliani, B. (2015), *Speed Leadership: A New Way to Lead for Rapidly Changing Times*, The CLBM LLC, Wethersfield, Connecticut

[3] Emiliani, B. and Torinesi, M. (2021), *Wheel of Fortune: Getting to the Heart of Business Strategy*, Cubic LLC, South Kingstown, Rhode Island

[4] Emiliani, B. (2022), *A Changed Perspective: An Essential Guide for Emerging Leaders*, Cubic LLC, South Kingstown, Rhode Island

[5] To learn how beliefs and untested assumptions, cognitive biases, illogical thinking, P-intelligence, and I-framing converge to create a huge corporate calamity, see Schiffer, Z. *et al.*, (2023), "Inside Elon's 'extremely hardcore' Twitter," *The Verge*, 17 January, https://www.theverge.com/23551060 /elon-musk-twitter-takeover-layoffs-workplace-salute-emoji, accessed 19 January 2023

[6] In our centuries-old economic system, survival and employment are synonymous.

[7] People crave the spectacle of performance, whether in sports, arts, business (i.e., leadership), or politics. It satisfies a vital spiritual need.

[8] For as long as the human species desires or requires spiritual provision, people will need leaders, and leaders will need the Institution of Leadership and the System of Profound Privilege due to its transcendent spiritual potency. It satisfies a uniquely human hunger for as long as it remains an evolutionary necessity.

About the Author

M.L. "Bob" Emiliani was a professor in the School of Engineering, Science, and Technology at Connecticut State University in New Britain, Conn., where he taught a graduate course on leadership, a unique course that analyzes failures in management decision-making, as well as other courses. He holds the honorary title of Professor Emeritus.

Bob earned a Bachelor of Science degree in mechanical engineering from the University of Miami, a Master of Science degree in chemical engineering from the University of Rhode Island, and a Doctor of Philosophy degree in engineering from Brown University.

He worked in the consumer products and aerospace industries for 15 years, beginning as a materials engineer. He has held management positions in engineering, manufacturing, and supply chain management at Pratt & Whitney. Bob joined academia in September 1999. While in academia, he developed a new teaching pedagogy and led activities to continuously improve master's degree programs.

Bob's curiosity led him to author or co-author 27 books, four book chapters, and more than 40 peer-reviewed papers in six different subject areas: leadership, management, management history, supply chain management, higher education, and materials engineering.

Please visit www.bobemiliani.com

I am truly honored when people take time
from their precious life to read my work.

Thank you.

♥ L

🙏 V

www.ingramcontent.com/pod-product-compliance
Lightning Source LLC
Chambersburg PA
CBHW031945190326
41519CB00007B/676